A New Dawn for Politics

T0024886

A New Dawn for Politics

Alain Badiou

Translated by Robin Mackay

polity

Originally published in French as *Les Possibles matins de la politique* by Alain Badiou © Librairie Arthème Fayard, 2021

This English edition © Polity Press, 2022

Polity Press
65 Bridge Street
Cambridge CB2 1UR, UK

Polity Press
111 River Street
Hoboken, NJ 07030, USA

ISBN-13: 978-1-5095-5300-6 (hardback)
ISBN-13: 978-1-5095-5301-3 (paperback)

A catalogue record for this book is available from the British Library.

Library of Congress Control Number: 2022935231

Typeset in 12.5 on 15 pt Adobe Garamond
by Fakenham Prepress Solutions, Fakenham, Norfolk NR21 8NL
Printed and bound in the UK by CPI Group (UK) Ltd, Croydon

The publisher has used its best endeavours to ensure that the URLs for external websites referred to in this book are correct and active at the time of going to press. However, the publisher has no responsibility for the websites and can make no guarantee that a site will remain live or that the content is or will remain appropriate.

Every effort has been made to trace all copyright holders, but if any have been overlooked the publisher will be pleased to include any necessary credits in any subsequent reprint or edition.

For further information on Polity, visit our website:
politybooks.com

Contents

Preface

The texts in this collection were conceived, written, and delivered between 2016 and 2020, for various purposes and in various locations. Revised, and where necessary amended, here they are given a kind of new lease of life. What all of them try to do, although not necessarily in a systematic way, is to talk about the present ideological and political situation, both in France and worldwide. The aim being not just to 'recount' the various news stories that make the headlines, whether in print, on the airwaves or on smartphones, but to arm ourselves with a few useful notions, largely the product of the last three hundred years, in order to understand what is going on. In doing so we must also keep in mind that the official 'news', a commodity placed on the market by a few billionaires, is itself part of 'what is going on', rather than being any aid to its comprehension.

The first part opens with some necessary general overviews. Contrary to empiricists, then, who think that the only way to understand a totality is by listing all of its elements and parts, I begin from afar, from a great distance, even though I am adamant that we can only comprehend what is going on right under our noses if we go to see it, and then only if we are active, activist even. We must be activists, but activists with a faculty of comprehension broadened and enlightened by long-term thinking. Symmetrically, contrary to dogmatists, who believe that everything depends upon what they have been taught to believe, my assertions will be guided not so much by existing states of affairs as by the gap, generally quite glaring, between the constraints imposed upon the future of societies and what could have been done, and still ought to be done, in order to overcome those constraints.

The first part of the book brings together essays that in some sense offer a 'bird's eye view', operating a dialectic of different epochs by examining what was constitutive of them, shedding light on their becomings and how they come to an end, and drawing some useful conclusions from these vicissitudes.

The second part, on the contrary, sets out from what is closest of all: those movements that have burst onto the scene, particularly in France, in recent years. It attempts to draw some lessons, both theoretical and practical, from these local adventures, in order to shed light upon what was misunderstood, to examine carefully what was proclaimed to be important, to point out what was neglected, and finally to prescribe what needs to be thought (the logic of Ideas) and done (the logic of activism) in order to bring about what I regard as, quite simply, the Good.

Alain Badiou
28 February 2021

Part I

Structures and Notions, Becomings and Visions

I

The Neolithic Age, Capitalism, and Communism

Let's start by being ambitious, in terms of both time and space. We shall go back to a few millennia before our own time and also, as is fashionable, we shall take a look at the fate of our beloved planet, revered by some contemporary believers under the name of the goddess Gaia.

It has become commonplace today to announce, for various reasons, that the end is nigh for the human species as we know it. From the typically messianic perspective of a certain brand of ecology, the predatory excesses of the evil animal that is the human being will soon bring about the end of the living world. And then, from the perspective of runaway techno-logical development we are told, in no particular order, of the takeover of all labour by robots, the sumptuous delights of the digital realm, automated art, deadly microplastics, and the threat of superhuman intelligence.

Consequently, we see the emergence of menacing categories such as transhumanism and the posthuman, or, in the other direction, a return to the animal, depending upon whether we listen to the prophecies of the tech industry or laments about the wounds inflicted on Mother Nature.

I regard all of these prophecies as so much ideological rhetoric designed to obscure the real danger facing humanity today, namely the impasse into which we are being led by globalised capitalism. It is in fact this social form, and it alone, which, wedded as it is to the pure notion of private profit, authorises the destructive exploitation of natural resources. That so many species are endangered, that the climate is still running out of control, that water is becoming a rare treasure – all of this is a by-product of the ruthless competition between predatory billionaires. And the fact that scientific development is anarchically enslaved to the imperative of producing saleable technologies has the same origin. Ecological preaching, which, despite its prophetic excesses, is often based on convincing descriptions, is in general becoming pure propaganda, useful to states that want to show everyone how caring they are, and transnational firms that, for the greater good of their turnover, are eager to make people believe in the noble and fraternal natural purity of the goods they traffic in.

Moreover, technological fetishism and the uninterrupted succession of 'revolutions' in this domain – the 'digital revolution' being currently the most fashionable – has constantly served to convince people that we are simultaneously heading for a workless paradise of helpful robots and universal laziness, and witnessing the human intellect being overtaken by electrical 'thought'. Today, not a magazine is published that does not present its astonished readers with the imminent 'victory' of artificial over natural intelligence. But in the majority of cases neither 'nature' nor 'artifice' are correctly or clearly defined.

Since the very origins of philosophy, it has often been asked what the word 'nature' means. It has meant the romantic reverie of sunsets, the atomic materialism of Lucretius (*De natura rerum*), the innermost being of all things, Spinoza's Totality

('Deus sive Natura'), the objective flipside of all culture, the countryside as opposed to the suspicious artifices of the city ('The earth does not lie', as Marshall Pétain said), biology as opposed to physics, the scope of cosmology as opposed to the minuscule neighbourhood of our planet, invariant tradition as opposed to frenzied innovation, natural sexuality as opposed to perversion …. Today, I'm afraid, 'nature' refers principally to nothing much more than the peace of gardens and villages, the touristic charms of wild animals, the beach, and the mountains where you might spend a pleasant summer. So who could possibly imagine that man is responsible for this Nature – man, who even now is nothing more than a thinking flea, hopping around on a secondary planet in a medium-sized solar system on the edge of a commonplace galaxy?

Since its origins, philosophy has also thought technics, or the arts. The ancient Greeks meditated on the dialectic of *technè* and *phusis*, situating the human animal within this dialectic and thus paving the way for the idea that the human is 'only a reed, the weakest in nature, but […] a thinking reed', which, according to Pascal, means: stronger than Nature, and closer to God. They long ago realised that the animal capable of mathematics would achieve great things in the material order. And are these 'robots' we hear so much about anything more than calculations assembled into the form of a machine, numbers crystallised into movements? They certainly count faster than we do, but it is we who designed them for precisely this task. Even if a crane can lift a huge concrete pole to a great height, it would be stupid to conclude from this that humans are incapable of doing so and that we are witnessing the birth of some muscular transhuman giant .... Similarly, counting at the speed of light is not a sign of unsurpassable 'intelligence'. Technological transhumanism just replays the same old trope, an inexhaustible theme in horror films and science fiction, of the creator outmanoeuvred by his creature, either so as to revel in the coming of the superman, which has been overdue since Nietzsche announced it, or to become fearful and take refuge under the skirts of Gaia or Mother Nature.

Let's get things into perspective.

For four or five thousand years now humanity has been organised by the triad of private property, which concentrates enormous wealth in the hands of tiny oligarchies, the family, in which wealth is passed on via inheritance, and the state, which protects both property and family by means of armed force. It is this triad that defined the Neolithic age of our species and we are still living in that age, indeed perhaps more so than ever. Capitalism is the contemporary form of the Neolithic: its enslaving of technics to competition, profit, and the concentration of capital only brings to an apotheosis the monstrous inequalities, social absurdities, military massacres and deleterious ideologies, which throughout the historical reign of the class hierarchy have always accompanied the deployment of new technologies.

It should be clear that technical inventions were the initial conditions for the arrival of the Neolithic Age, not its result. Looking at the fate of our own animal species, we can see that sedentary agriculture, the domestication of cattle and horses, pottery, bronze, metal weapons, writing, nationhood, monumental architecture, and monotheistic religions are inventions at least as important as the aeroplane and the smartphone. What is human in history has always been artificial by definition, otherwise the humanity we know, Neolithic humanity, would not exist, but only a humanity that was still close to the animal realm – something that did indeed continue to exist in the form of small nomadic groups for around two hundred thousand years.

Fearful, obscurantist primitivism has its roots in the fallacious concept of 'primitive communism'. Today it takes the form of a cultic belief in friendly archaic societies where babies, women, men, and old people lived fraternally along with mice, frogs, and bears. Ultimately, all of this is nothing more than ridiculous reactive propaganda, since everything points towards the fact that the societies in question were extremely violent, constantly labouring under the yoke of necessity, just struggling to survive.

Moreover, to talk today in hushed tones of the victory of the artificial over the natural, of the robot over the human, is a ridiculously regressive point of view, a real absurdity. Our reply to these terrors and prophecies should be as follows: a simple axe, or a trained horse, to say nothing of a papyrus full of signs, are already exemplary trans- or posthuman items; the abacus already made it possible to calculate much faster than with the fingers of the hand.

The question of our time is certainly not that of a return to primitivism or a messianic terror in the face of the 'ravages' of technology, nor is it that of a morbid fascination with the science fiction of all-conquering robots. The real task before us is to make a methodical and urgent exit from the Neolithic. This millennial order, which values only competition and hierarchy and tolerates the misery of billions of human beings, must be overcome at all costs, before we witness the unleashing of more of those wars that have been the preserve of the Neolithic since its emergence, technologised conflicts in the lineage of the two World Wars of 1914–18 and 1939–45, in which tens of millions died. This time it could be many more.

The issue is not technology or nature, but the organisation of societies on a global scale. It is about insisting that a non-Neolithic social organisation is possible, meaning: no private ownership of what should be common, i.e. the production of everything necessary for human life, and everything that makes it worthwhile. No family inheritances, no concentration of wealth.

No separate state to protect the oligarchies. No hierarchical division of labour. No nations, no closed and mutually hostile identities. Collective organisation of everything pertaining to the collective interest.

All of this has a name, a fine name: communism. Capitalism is only the ultimate phase of the restrictions that the Neolithic form of society has imposed upon human life, the final stage of the Neolithic. *Encore un effort*, fine human animal, to break out of a condition that has seen five thousand years of inventiveness benefiting only a small handful of people. For almost two centuries, since Marx at any rate, we have known that the new age must begin, the age of unprecedented technologies for all, of work distributed equally to all, of the sharing of everything and of education that affirms the genius of all. In short, this new communism must oppose, everywhere and in all matters, the morbid survival of capitalism, this supposed 'modernity' of a world that in reality has already been around for five thousand years, which makes it old, far too old.

2

The Notion of 'Crisis'

True and False Contradictions of the Contemporary World

A great deal is being written today, in the most servile prose, about the 'crisis', the 'state of crisis', the threat of 'the Crisis'. The crisis is always to blame, whether it's a hack writing to order or an exasperated protestor, the one enumerating an arsenal of measures to avoid or end this supposed 'crisis', the other believing that they glimpse revolution already looming on the other side of the crisis. At a fundamental level, modernity and the contemporary inevitably expose us to crises that will likely become ever more anarchic and insurmountable in the future, something the hack worries about and the leftist rejoices in.

So let's start with modernity, with the essential forms of the contemporary world.

First of all, modernity is a negative reality, for it stands for the exit from tradition. It spells the end of the old world of castes, nobility, religious obligation, initiation rites, local mythologies, the subjugation of women, the absolute power of the father over his sons, the official separation between a small number of powerful people and the despised working masses. There is no going back on this movement, which undoubtedly began in the West as early as the Renaissance, was consolidated by the Enlightenment in the eighteenth century, and has since been materially realised by the unprecedented development of techniques of production and the incessant improvement of the means of calculation, circulation, and communication.

Perhaps the most striking point to be made here is that this exit from the world of tradition, this veritable tornado, which has made its way through humanity, taking barely three centuries to sweep away forms of organisation that had lasted for millennia, occasioned a subjective crisis the causes and true extent of which we are only beginning to perceive today. One of the most obvious aspects of it is the increasing difficulty that young people face in situating themselves within this new world without succumbing to a stark alternative: either participate in the festivities of capital or roam aimlessly, lost to an overwhelming nihilism.

This is the real crisis. It is sometimes said that its cause is the advent of financial capitalism. But in fact it should be noted first of all that this capitalism is in full global expansion, that it is doing wonderfully well. Crises and wars? They are part of its particular mode of development. These are the means, savage but necessary, by which it purges competition and makes sure that the greatest possible quantity of available capital is concentrated in the winners' hands. All of this is governed by the most fundamental law of all: the law of the concentration of capital.

From this strictly objective point of view – that of the concentration of capital – let us recall where we stand today. Today, one per cent of the world's population owns 46 per cent of the available capital, with 10 per cent of that group owning 86 per cent of that proportion. And then 50 per cent of the population of the world owns exactly nothing: zero per cent. Which leaves 14 per cent. Understandably, the 10 per cent who own almost everything are not at all eager to mix with those who have nothing. And, in turn, many of those who share the meagre 14 per cent left over once the rich have helped themselves are ferociously keen to hold on to what they have. This is why, so often, with the help of racism and nationalism, they throw their support behind countless repressive bulwarks against the terrible 'threat' they see embodied in the 50 per cent who have nothing.

All of this means that the supposedly unifying slogan of the Occupy Wall Street movement, 'We are the 99 per cent', rang perfectly hollow. The truth is that the so-called 'West' is full of people who, while not included in the 10 per cent of the ruling aristocracy, nonetheless provide globalised capitalism with its petty-bourgeois band of supporters, the so-called 'middle classes' without whom the 'democratic' order would have no chance of surviving. Which means that, far from being 'the 99 per cent', even symbolically, the courageous young people of Wall Street, even in regard to their origin, represented only a small handful of people, sure to fade away once the festivities of the 'movement' die down. Unless, of course, they create more sustained links with the real mass of those who have nothing or very little, thus tracing a political diagonal between those of the 14 per cent, especially the intellectuals, and those of the 50 per cent, first of all workers and peasants, and then the lower orders of the middle classes, those who are poorly paid and precarious. This is an entirely feasible political path, one that was tried in the 1960s and 1970s under the auspices of Maoism. And it has been tried once again recently by the occupation movement in Tunis and Cairo, and even in Oakland, where an active link with dockworkers in the port was at least attempted. Everything, absolutely everything, depends upon the definitive revival of this alliance and its political organisation on an international scale.

However, in the extremely weakened state in which this movement finds itself today, the objective appreciable result of the exit from tradition, so long as it takes place under the auspices of the globalised formalism of capital, can be nothing other than what we have just described, namely a tiny oligarchy dictating its law not only to the overwhelming majority on the edge of mere survival, but also to the westernised, i.e. vassalised and politically sterile, middle classes.

What is going on at the social and subjective level? In 1848 Marx described it in a way that is most striking, in that it rings infinitely more true today than it did in his own times. Let us quote a few lines from this old text, which is still incredibly fresh today:

> The bourgeoisie, wherever it has got the upper hand, has put an end to all feudal, patriarchal, idyllic relations. [...] It has drowned the most heavenly ecstasies of religious fervour, of chivalrous enthusiasm, of philistine sentimentalism, in the icy water of egotistical calculation. It has resolved personal worth into exchange value. [...] The bourgeoisie has stripped of its halo every occupation hitherto honoured and looked up to with reverent awe. It has converted the physician, the lawyer, the priest, the poet, the man of science, into its paid wage labourers.

What Marx is describing here is how the exit from tradition, in its bourgeois capitalist version, has in fact unleashed a gigantic crisis in the symbolic organisation of humanity. For thousands of years the differences internal to human life have been coded and symbolised in hierarchical form. The most important dualities – young and old,

17

woman and man, who is in my family and who is not, the wretched and the powerful, my professional group and other groups, foreigners and natives, heretics and the faithful, commoners and noblemen, town and country, intellectuals and manual workers – were dealt with, in language, mythologies, ideologies, and established religious moralities, through the use of ordering structures that coded the place of every person within a set of nested hierarchies. A noblewoman was inferior to her husband but superior to a common man; a rich bourgeois had to bow to a duke but his servants had to bow to him; and a Native American woman was almost nothing compared to a warrior of her tribe, but almost everything compared to a prisoner from another tribe. A poverty-stricken follower of the Catholic Church was a negligible figure in the eyes of his bishop, but could be considered a chosen one in the eyes of a Protestant heretic, just as the son of a freeman was absolutely dependent upon his father but could have as his personal slave a black man who was father to a large family.

All of this traditional symbolisation is based on a structure of order that distributes the places and consequently the relations between those places. Now, the exit from tradition, in the form in which it is realised by capitalism as a general system of production, does not really offer any active new symbolisation, but only the brutal and independent functioning of the economy, the neutral, asymbolic reign of what Marx calls 'the icy water of egotistical calculation'. The result is a historical crisis of symbolisation that brings about great disorientation for the youth of today.

In the face of this crisis, which, in the guise of a neutral freedom, proposes money as the only universal reference, we are led to believe that there are only two paths available today. Either the affirmation that there is and can be nothing better than this liberal and 'democratic' model, its freedoms constrained by the neutrality of market calculation; or the reactive desire for a return to tradition, i.e. to hierarchical symbolisation.

In my view, both paths lead to extremely dangerous dead ends, and the increasingly violent conflict between them can only draw humanity into an endless cycle of conflict. This is the whole problem of false contradictions, which serve to prevent the play of true contradiction. For the true contradiction, the one that ought to serve as a reference point for thought and action, is the one that opposes two different visions of the inevitable exit from the hierarchical symbolic tradition: *the asymbolic vision of Western capitalism, which creates monstrous inequalities and pathogenic errancies, and the vision generally known as 'communism', which since the time of Marx and his contemporaries has proposed the invention of an egalitarian symbolisation.* Following the historical collapse of state socialism in the USSR and in China, this fundamental contradiction of the modern world has been masked by a false contradiction, the contradiction which – in the face of the exit from tradition – *sets the purely neutral and sterile negativity of the dominating West in opposition to fascistic reaction,* a reaction which, often draped in bastardised religious narratives and with a spectacular violence designed to conceal its real impotence, advocates the return to the old hierarchies.

This differend serves the interests of both sides, however violent their conflict may appear. With the help of the media, it captures the general public interest, forcing everyone to make a false choice such as 'the West or barbarism' or, even more stupidly, 'Republican secularism or Islamic terrorism', thus blocking the advent of the only global conviction that could save humanity from disaster. This conviction – old Platonist that I am, I sometimes call it the 'Communist Idea' – states that, in the very same movement by which we exit tradition, we must work towards the invention of an egalitarian symbolism capable of guiding, encoding, and forming the peaceful subjective substrate for the collectivisation of resources, the effective disappearance of inequalities, the recognition of differences with equal subjective rights, and, ultimately, the decline of separate state authorities.

We must therefore place our subjectivity in the service of an entirely new task: the invention, in a struggle that must be fought on two fronts – against the ruination of the symbolic in the icy waters of capitalist calculation and against the reactive fascism that dreams of restoring the old order – for an egalitarian symbolisation that reinstates differences under the auspices of common rules, themselves derived from a generalised sharing of resources.

As far as we in the West are concerned, we must first of all bring about a Cultural Revolution, ridding ourselves of the absolutely archaic conviction that our vision of things is superior to all others. On the contrary, it lags far behind what the first great critics of the unequal and meaningless brutality of capitalism already looked forward to and called for as early as the nineteenth century. These great pioneers also saw that supposedly democratic political organis-ation, with its ridiculous electoral rituals, was only a screen for the total subjugation of politics by the higher interests of competition and greed. Today more than ever, we have before our eyes the sad spectacle of what, with their merciless lucidity, they called 'parliamentary cretinism'.

The full-scale abandonment of this 'Western' identity, together with the absolute rejection of reactive fascisms, constitutes the obligatory negative stage in the wake of which we will be able to assert the power of new egalitarian values. No longer being the plaything of false contradiction, but instead installing ourselves in the true contradiction, will alter subjectivities and finally render them capable of inventing the political force that will replace private property and competition with what Marx called 'free association'.

3

Science, Ideology, and the Middle Class

'Ideology' is one of the most disputed and obscure terms in the vocabulary of Marxism, and that of political thought in general. We can still say, with Marx, that 'ideology' names the set of dominant opinions and values proper to each of the social classes that make up a society. For classical Marxism, ideology 'in itself' means nothing: ideology is always the ideology of a given social class. More precisely, ideology is the subjective effect of social objectivity: convictions, ways of thinking, relationships to family and state, religion – all of these go to make up ideology, as a consequence of the position of a class within the contradictory whole that every society is. And since for Marx the very essence of social objectivity, at least until the advent of communism, consists in division and conflict, ideology is the subjective level of an objectivity fundamentally divided by class struggle.

But if ideology is the subjective level of opinions and values of the social classes, and if the objective world is divided, then we must speak not of one ideology but of at least two – two opposing ideologies. Ideology is a dialectical concept, meaning that the real is represented in the ideological figure of a conflict between bourgeois ideology, the dominant ideology in the world today, and proletarian ideology, which is the main ideology of the dominated. It could also be said that what we have in the sphere of political representations is, on the side of domination, a conservative ideology that protects this domination and, on the side of the dominated, a revolutionary ideology that aims to destroy the existing social order.

Historically, at the most general level, according to the 'marxisant' view of ideology, what we have had for two short centuries is something like capitalism on the one hand and communism or its weak variant, socialism, on the other. So ultimately we are dealing with two largely stabilised world views. It is not simply a conflict of opinions, but a major conflict between two antagonistic visions of the social order as such. This was how communist parties and classical Marxism saw things between the 1840s and 1970s.

As is well known, things began to change in the 1960s when classical communism, centred on the USSR, began to unravel. It was then that Louis Althusser, a member of the PCF, proposed a new interpretation of the word 'ideology'. Of course, the dominant ideology is still opposed to the proletarian ideology, but Althusser introduces the idea that as well as this simple contradiction, there is also *an opposition between ideology 'in general' and science.* Consequently, the concept of ideology can be constructed in two stages: firstly on the basis of the essential difference between 'ideological thought' and 'scientific thought', and then by dividing 'ideological thought' into 'proletarian ideology' and 'bourgeois ideology'.

For Althusser, ideology is an imaginary representation of the real world, whereas science is a conceptual knowledge that makes it possible to think the real of that world. Philosophically, what results is a contradiction between two different contradictions. The first contradiction, between ideology and science, is a contradiction between particularity and universality, whereas the second contradiction sets into opposition two particularities, that of the ideology of the bourgeoisie and that of the ideology of the proletariat.

We are dealing with a complex dialectical apparatus here. The problem is how to construct a unity between the two contradictions, the contradiction between universality and particularity and the contradiction between two particularities. Althusser's intriguing but problematic proposal is that proletarian, revolutionary ideology, which, as a communist, he believes is the *right* ideology, is closely related to science, and that there is therefore something more universal in proletarian ideology than in bourgeois ideology. The conservative ideology of the bourgeoisie, after all, is closely linked not to the universality of science but to particular idealistic constructs such as religion, the pseudo-freedom of trade, and the creative value of private enterprise. Thus, the right ideology – the revolutionary proletarian ideology, ultimately communism – is seen as a historically unprecedented relation between the particularity of a class ideology (that of the proletariat) and its apparent opposite, the universality of science. As a result, the class struggle at the ideological level, which at first appears as a conflict between two particularities, turns out to bear within itself a contradiction between particularity and universality. In short, if proletarian ideology is the 'right ideology', it is not only because it is the ideology of the workers, of revolutionaries, of the poor, against bourgeois domination, but also, more fundamentally, because it is an ideology that is on the side of universality.

This complex situation has a number of consequences. One is that the decision as to which, ultimately, is the right ideology, the progressive ideology, the ideology of the future, of the historical future, is not to be made only on the level of the concrete conflicts between classes, but also that of the metaphysical conflict between particularity and universality. Which is why, in the end, class conflict can also be said to be the organising principle of philosophy. First there is the conflict between two socially and culturally different classes, and then something like a more abstract conflict between particularity and universality, and then finally, Althusser concludes, a philosophical conflict, namely an ideological struggle between idealism, on the side of ideology without universality, and materialism, on the side of science, i.e. ultimately, on the side of an ideology that stands in an immanent relation to the universality of science.

What is the thinking today on all of these questions?

As has been eagerly pointed out in objection to Althusser, much of capitalist ideology is clearly on the side of a certain kind of materialism. In our society, dominated by capitalist organisation, the goal of existence is a life that is as pleasant as possible, a life that affords you the greatest possible quantity of material and social, empirical and symbolic satisfactions: on the side of desires and needs, the satisfaction of having the means to buy what you like, houses, cars, holidays, etc., and therefore to have a decent 'standard of living' in the material sense. And then to have a good and fulfilling place in the hierarchies of the social world, to be saved from the perils of errant destitution, or of a job that has no social cachet. All of this is defined relative to the good places available in society as it is, and has no idealistic grandeur to it. From this point of view, the dominant ideology of the capitalist world is undoubtedly materialism. Let us add that material satisfaction and symbolic vanity, which are the common norms in this type of society, are closely linked to the circulation of money. With money you can access the global market, the universal market, and find multiple possibilities for personal satisfaction. But no matter how abstract it may seem, money cannot reasonably be considered to be a figure of idealism! It always operates on the side of what Marx calls 'the icy water of egotistical calculation'. In a sense, mediaeval chivalry was far more idealistic than the CAC40 stock market index, which today brings together the leaders of French capital.

As a result, Althusser's conclusion that the ideological contradiction is between materialism on the side of the proletariat and idealism on the side of the bourgeoisie is quite probably incorrect. And, if this is the case, it is because the problem of ideology is more complex than he said it was.

Indeed, we can see today that proletarian ideology, revolutionary and communist ideas, have taken on a character that, at least in terms of their real historical appearance, seems largely idealist. Looking at the world as it is today, we may well conclude that there is indeed a conflict between materialism and idealism, but we would be strongly tempted to place the bourgeoisie on the side of a kind of almost obscene relentless materialism, and revolutionaries, to say nothing of communists – an endangered species, I know because I'm one of them! – on the side of idealism.

Althusser placed science on the side of proletarian ideology. However, through the mediation of technology and sophisticated material production, science today appears to have succumbed to capitalist domination and seems to have practically no constituted link with communism. We thus seem to have shifted from Althusser's philosophical position to its pure and simple opposite: materialism on the side of the bourgeoisie, idealism on the side of the proletariat and the revolution.

What, then, is the real question underlying this strange story? I think the difficulty stems from the fact that, in this historical view of ideological conflict, all that is taken into account is the pairing of two pairs: bourgeoisie and proletariat on the one hand, materialism and idealism on the other. But today we are witnessing the development of a very large middle class. It is no longer enough to describe the contemporary world in terms of a simple conflict between bourgeoisie and proletariat. In a certain sense, the middle class is now the decisive class in terms of political determination. It represents the greatest number and it serves to defend the capitalist order. Counting to two is no longer enough: you have to count to three.

Here are a few figures, to which I return obsessively, but for a purpose other than simply describing inequalities: in the contemporary world, 10 per cent of the global population owns 86 per cent of global wealth. We thus have, on a purely economic level, a very small dominant group, 10 per cent of the population. It is no exaggeration to call it an oligarchy. On the other hand, 50 per cent of the world population owns absolutely none of the global wealth. These can be called the proletarian masses, a term that has always referred to the class that has nothing. These proletarian masses consist not only of workers: the masses are no longer identical with the working class, they also include a huge number of people who have nothing, who have, in a sense, no access to the opportunities of the world as it is: no access to work, to money or, ultimately, to the market. That leaves the 40 per cent of people who, worldwide, own 14 per cent of the global wealth. This is the middle class. It couldn't be clearer: 10 per cent, the dominant group; 50 per cent, the global mass with nothing; and 40 per cent, the middle class.

You can see immediately that these figures force us to pose the question of ideology no longer in relation to two terms, but inevitably in relation to three: the dominant group, the great masses with nothing (which is what 'proletarian' means: having only oneself to sell), and the middle class. We have a financial, commercial, and industrial oligarchy, the mass of proles, and the modern middle class. The latter is largely concentrated in the Western world, if by 'Western world' we understand those countries with a strongly capitalist structure and an imperial tendency: Europe, North America, and Japan. The question then becomes: What is the ideological disposition of the middle class?

This is the great enigma of today's world. What exactly is the ideological outlook of the middle class? I think it consists in two elements, so it's not a simple disposition, but a contradictory one. The first element is that – quite clearly today, but not necessarily forever – the middle class essentially accepts the domination of capitalism and therefore accepts the power of money and the historical triumph of a very small oligarchy. But only subject to certain conditions, primarily concerning individual freedom and its many consequences: freedom of opinion, at least in the form of personal convictions and chatter; freedom of trade, at least subject to the control of the large industrial and agricultural companies and their accomplices in the banking world; the possibility of free movement, subject to a minimum income. We can also see that the middle class accepts the global domination of capitalism so long as, locally, there is some kind of state that provides it with a channel to complain, rant, criticise, and even – supreme happiness – vote, provided this has no noticeable effect on the general form of society. These capitalist states that domesticate the middle class are called 'democracies'.

It is very important to form a clear idea on this point. There is acceptance of the domination of capital, of its concentration in the hands of a small oligarchy, on condition that there is a democratic-type state at the local level where one lives. So it's a question of a relationship between the global situation and the local situation. I call this relationship *democratic materialism*. 'Materialism' because it involves acceptance of the material structure of the world, 'democratic' because this acceptance is made on condition of freedom of opinion [*opinion*], or, we might say, freedom to consent [*opiner*], along with all of its mediocre consequences. This is the first element of the middle-class ideology.

The second element is that the middle class is keen not to be confused with the great masses of the very poor. It accepts oligarchic-monetary domination, but demands that a distance be maintained between it and the huge masses of those who have nothing at all. As a result, when there is a crisis of capitalism, a kind of crisis of domination (as happened in Europe around 2008), the middle class gets spooked: afraid of being degraded and belittled, it is thrown into a kind of disorder that manifests itself in various forms, including a tendency towards aggression against minorities, foreigners, nomads, and so on.

This is what I would call *conservative materialism*, by which I mean the middle class's desperate need to be reassured of its status, and, above all, not to be confused with the poor masses.

In order to fully describe the ideological situation of the middle class today, we must posit, first, a background that is materialist in nature: a modern materialism that consists in the acceptance of capitalism and of the global power of a small oligarchy. And then a contradiction between this democratic materialism and a conservative materialism, dominated by the fear of being confused with the great masses of the poor. This is the only clear explanation of the democratic structure of modern states. Indeed, in our modern democratic states there are usually two parties: democrats and republicans, conservatives and labour, or, more generally, Left and Right. This mode of political organisation reflects the ambivalence of the middle class, caught between the fear of being confused with the proletarians of the world, which is what drives the Right, the party of conservative materialism, and the pseudo-reforming acceptance of a reasonable cohabitation with the capitalist oligarchy on condition that 'human rights' are respected, which is what drives the Left, the party of democratic materialism. Political power lies within this opposition between democratic materialism and conservative materialism, which ultimately defines the ideological structure of the middle class, i.e. that of almost 40 per cent of the world's population, who between them own 14 per cent of the world's wealth. Thus, the political field of 'democracies' is not strictly speaking that of an ideological struggle, because there are not really two different ideologies at play here: everything takes place within the same materialism, at the cost of its taking on two different inflections, which take turns in directing the state. Or, as Marx said: the two families of Capital's middle-managers.

Our problem then becomes: Is anything like a real ideological struggle going on here?

In order for there to be a real ideological struggle, it is necessary that there be an ideology that is external to the dominant materialism, whatever its inflection, conservative or democratic. Thus, the real political question is not and cannot be the purely formal contradiction that defines 'democracy' in the field of state power. What is needed is an orientation of thought that cannot be reduced to the conflict between democratic and conservative materialisms. What is needed is a politics whose ideology consists in accepting neither the domination of the small oligarchy nor the forms of materialism of which it approves. And which, therefore, refuses the 'democratic' temptation of the electoral bazaar and genuflection before the freedom to assent. We must follow certain revolutionaries of the past in arguing that participation in elections, which always just means having the middle class divide itself between two materialisms, neither of which aims at the destruction of the established capitalist order, ultimately amounts to nothing more than 'parliamentary cretinism'.

At this point, where all the difficulty is concentrated, it is useful to look back at terrible events that have recently affected our country. I am talking about the terrifying mass murder that took place in the heart of Paris. How do you explain, how do you give a rational interpretation of something that is inherently irrational, as is always the case with the murder of people who just happen to be there, who the killers don't know, whose thoughts they know nothing of? It's a mass murder that at first sight seems to be aimless and meaningless. On the other hand, at the symbolic level it is perfectly clear that it can be interpreted as the murder of the Western middle class, the desire to kill the middle class whether 'democratic' or 'conservative'. The very place chosen by the killers bears witness to this: the Bataclan is a nightclub for the entertainment of the lower middle class – not the rich middle class, but the middle class of ordinary people, especially the young. It is about destroying the middle class of the Western world. This is also the reason for choosing Paris, as a symbol of the (cultural) values of the Western world. But why?

It is important to realise that today, being outside the oligarchic system that the West lays claim to means being outside the middle class. At the same time, however, there is a subjective conviction that being outside the middle class is in some sense necessary and yet impossible. Indeed, the killers are by no means communists. They even secretly aspire to the Western status of the middle class. The only possible relationship with the middle class is to destroy it, and thus to kill anyone who is a symbol of the 'middle', even if it means killing themselves. As we know, the majority of these attacks end with the suicide of their perpetrators. '*Viva la muerte*', as the fascists in Spain said – an indiscriminate '*muerte*' of others and of myself.

What we are dealing with here is a conflict between two visions of our world. First of all, we must not lose sight of the obvious, which is that the middle class is a creation of modern capitalism. On the other hand, the existence of a division between a small oligarchy and a mass of people who have nothing is a very old situation: 10 per cent of the population is the same proportion as the nobility in France in the seventeenth century. So this difference is not new. But the positive novelty, the creation of the modern world, is this middle class with all its ambiguities, all its internal divisions. The middle class has become the symbol of capitalist modernity.

But what if you don't want to play the 'democratic' game, or claim not to want to, at least in so far as it presupposes the indefinite acceptance of capitalist power? What if you refuse to inscribe yourself in the Right/Left division that governs political opinions under the regime of bourgeois dictatorship camouflaged by parliamentarianism?

Then there are only three possibilities. Either you try to 'toughen up' the democratic half of bourgeois materialism by electing a few 'communists' who will make an audible but ineffective noise within the indestructible official institutions of capital. See the action of the French Communist Party (PCF) or the Trotskyite sects. This is the 'entryist' line: declare yourself to be outside, but go in anyway. Or else, like the killers, with mass murders that end in your own suicide, you symbolically enact a phantasmatic killing of the middle class and, ultimately, of the entire West. This is the 'ultra-leftist' line: your ostensible exteriority is the interiority of death. Or else, finally, abandoning any desire you might have for 'democratic' participation in the secondary trappings of bourgeois power, and thus refusing wholesale to inscribe yourself in the division of bourgeois materialism between Right and Left, you work towards the emergence of a political logic that is totally external, at all levels of its deployment, to that proposed by the 'democracies'. This is the 'new communism' line. You then try to bring the proletarians into this creative endeavour, of course, but also a significant part of the middle class.

The political problem is not at all one of creating, in the face of the subordination of the middle class to capital, a purely destructive exterior. Nor is it to be inside and nothing else, i.e. to accept for all eternity the classic situation with alternating democratic materialism and conservative materialism – one day it's the Right, next day it's the Left. The true way is to divide the middle class, to create a contradiction within it, to work on rallying the outside from inside, and therefore, contrary to all entryism, to propose a logic of exit and autonomy from without.

So I would define politics, real politics, which is neither conservative politics nor classical democratic politics, as the attempt to induce a certain segment of the middle class to come onto the side of the masses of poor people who are on the outside, overcoming the fear of losing their own status; to convince a segment of the middle class that real modernity consists in going beyond the continual oscillation between democratic materialism and conservative materialism. One must have the courage to go outside, to see the outside, to understand the people outside, to be with them, so as to create, for a part of the middle class itself, not a destructive pure outside but a new possibility, that of actively refusing the domination of a small oligarchy. It is a question of separating the democratic element from its capitalist foundation, of isolating it from its capitalist background.

Philosophically, this amounts to the creation of a new materialism. We no longer deal with the contradiction between materialism and idealism, but with the contradiction between two different materialisms. To create a communist materialism in the contemporary situation certainly means to create a materialism, but one without the oligarchy and without the monstrous power of the small financial, commercial, and industrial group. We may interpret the terrible nihilistic mass murders as an expression of the impossibility of creating something outside capable of rallying a significant fraction of those inside, the impossibility of inventing a new materialism, one that consists of creating, for the best subjects of the middle class, *the possibility of going from the inside to the outside.*

I have called this possibility *dialectical materialism*, and you can understand why. It is a materialism that results from a contradiction within itself, because it disjoins the two components of democratic materialism, separating the democratic element from the conservative element. Philosophically, this is a new question in relation to the contemporary political world, or in any case absolutely new in relation to the death drive of terrorism and mass murders. This invention of a dialectical materialism is really something new, not only in relation to terrorism, to the death drive, to the fiction of the pure outside, but also in relation to conservative power as such. The question is that of turning the Idea of Equality – the idea of a world without any ruling oligarchy, an idea that opposes the conservative part of the ruling materialism – into a materialist power, that of a new materialism, dialectical materialism.

We can therefore propose a conclusion to our problem, which was that of contemporary ideology. We saw first of all that, at the ideological level, we had the opposition of two terms, bourgeoisie and proletariat. Then we saw that at the philosophical level the contradiction was between materialism and idealism. Finally, we find ourselves faced with the contradiction between two materialisms. But this contradiction between two materialisms – *state materialism*, internal to capitalism, with its two components (conservative and democratic) and *dialectical materialism*, an organic movement on the outside – is a contradiction that remains to be constructed. Indeed, it is not a contradiction of the world as it is, it is a contradiction that must be invented and inscribed in the concrete world by separating what today is unified. It is a question of opening a proletarian door to the middle class by liberating democracy from its coupling, via conservative materialism, with the dominant oligarchy, and tracing from this door the political path of a long-term practicable historical outside, totally distinct from both ultra-leftist turmoil and suicidal strife.

4

Lecture at the Institute of Political Sciences

I would of course like to thank the Union of Communist Students for having invited me to what is a kind of academic temple of modern parliamentarianism.

But how can I justify the legitimacy of this invitation? In any case, I cannot, here in this Institute of Political Studies in Paris, otherwise known as 'Sciences Po', speak as a specialist in political science or political studies. I certainly believe that there are political truths, but not that there can be such a thing as 'political studies' a political science or sciences, or sciences of politics, and even less so a scientific politics. When you read the discourse that goes by these names, you find three things, and three things only.

Firstly, carefully formatted political opinions, so that what results from choices and decisions is disguised as the result of an objective analysis with a universal status. Secondly, a few rudiments of economics and law, neither of which is a science, and which have only an indirect (if important) relationship to politics proper. And, finally, a little history of political ideologies and philosophical arguments relating to politics. All of this really serves to prepare one for the management of public affairs, affairs of state. And, indeed, the political Gotha, the arsenal of those in power, in all parts of the French state from its public staging to its obscure backstage areas, is largely drawn from the Institute of Political Studies, and, if I may say so, in particular from its top floor, the National School of Administration. The fact that these institutions attach or glue the word 'politics' to the word 'administration', as if the two were one and the same, can indicate only one thing: 'politics' means 'management of the affairs of the state'. This amounts to depriving it of any true universal status and of any status as a principle for collective action.

Allow me to make a remark in passing here: the expression 'the sphere of politics [*le politique*]', which crops up regularly in the fake discipline known as 'political philosophy', seems to me to be devoid of all meaning. What exists is the political [*la politique*], or more precisely, a plurality of political stances [*politiques*]. The political is the space of the conflict of political stances. So, when there is only one political stance, there are in fact none, but only affairs of state, management, and administration. In the current parliamentary system, to claim that there are several political stances would clearly be a fiction. There is really only one, entirely subordinated to the consensual doublet of the electoral representative system and liberal capitalism, which I propose we call capitalo-parliamentarianism. And since there is only one political stance, namely capitalo-parliamentarism, there are none, and there is no politics. An increasing number of people realise this, which is why they end up converting to total political scepticism.

If I were to yield to my usual polemical daimon, I would be liable to say that an Institute of Political Studies, let alone of political sciences, is and can only be a school of managerial depoliticisation. But I am prevented from doing so by the knowledge that a number of those who attend this school, including, I suppose, those who have invited me here, are precisely trying to fight against this kind of administrative neutralisation of political engagement.

In any case, 'political sciences' aside, I must begin by defining the place, intellectual and practical, from which I speak to you.

First of all, of course, there is philosophy. I maintain that the conceptual inventiveness of philosophy is conditional upon other modes of thought, other practices. Philosophy is not a radical beginning, but rather a consequence. As Hegel tells us, 'the owl of Minerva flies at dusk'. And politics is one of these conditions, both the contemporary political real and the history of politics. As such, any political novelty that may manifest itself in the world today is of interest to the philosopher. And since I have been asked to talk about communism, obviously I must add that I speak under the historical condition of the near-disappearance of everything this word once represented. I mean the collapse of the Soviet Union; the incorporation of the Central European countries into the purely capitalist space called 'Europe'; the aggressive capitalist development of China following the failure of the Cultural Revolution; the decline of all communist parties in all countries, including France, where the party had been prosperous for a long time, and last but not least the criminalisation of the very word 'communism', condemned without trial to be identified solely with the Terror, with massacres, concentration camps and, in a kind of symmetry of 'Evil Empires', with Nazism.

That is to say, if the claim is to speak of communism, to really speak of it and not just pretend, today Hegel's philosophical owl has flown away entirely into the dark night of a moral panic, chased by the jeers of those who know that the term 'communism' is to be discarded into the pit of those words that are both dated and accursed.

However, can it not at least be argued that the complete collapse of a political and state apparatus that was a worldwide presence and was still very powerful less than fifty years ago, poses a real question to our thinking? That there is an enigma here that remains unresolved?

Here I can set out once again from philosophy, my own philosophy. For me, all truth, i.e. everything that has a verifiable universal scope, originates, is created, within a particular historical context. I might even go so far as to say that this is the most important philosophical problem I deal with.

How can we understand the idea that something with a universal status can nonetheless begin, be created in and deployed from, situations that are always absolutely particular in both space and time, geographically and historically? How can we account for the fact that demonstrative mathematics, which today is identical everywhere in terms of its protocol, and is recognised everywhere as having universal validity, was invented in Greece between the second or third centuries BCE? But equally, how can we explain the extraordinary effect on a modern French reader of a book like *The Tale of Genji*, written a thousand years ago by a Japanese aristocrat? Or again, how is it that the character of Robespierre, an eighteenth-century enlightenment bourgeois figure, is still an object of study and still arouses contradictory passions today? Or that the love letters between Heloise and Abelard, a typical product of the mediaeval world, can still touch our hearts? In other words, how can something of universal value have an absolutely particular beginning in space and time?

This kind of beginning of what is universal in a particular world is what I call an 'event'. It follows that, as a philosopher, I am interested in anything that resembles an event in this sense, everything that seems to produce effects that, although localised, could prove universal in their scope.

I may then at least pose the following question: Is the collapse, within the space of a few years, of everything that went by the name of 'communism' related in some way or another to an event? You'll tell me: it was just a failure pure and simple. But failures can be very important events. The Paris Commune of 1871 was a terrible and bloody failure. Nonetheless, since it was the first workers' insurrection that had succeeded in seizing power in a major capital city, even if only for a few weeks, the Paris Commune is a political event that is still a subject of reflection today, to the extent that in February 2021 its commemoration is still being violently debated in the Council of Paris. The Cultural Revolution in China, between 1966 and 1976, was also a total and terribly costly failure. But I could demonstrate here, although I will not do so today, that it was such a complex and rich event that it is only now that we are starting to really think it through and draw its consequences. In fact, I have suggested that we consider the Chinese Cultural Revolution as the Paris Commune of the era of powerful socialist states.

Ultimately, my question is as follows: Is what has taken place in the second half of the twentieth century and up to the present day in all the countries that regarded the system of popular democracy as a step towards communism, and in all the parties inspired by this experiment, an event from which consequences can be drawn that have a universal status? Or is it a catastrophe as bloody as it was predictable, from which we can learn nothing?

The methodological point to consider first of all is the following: an event cannot have a universal status if it is solely negative. Or, more precisely, if it consists only in destroying one situation to replace it with another situation that is already perfectly known and established. For an event is a creation, a novelty for thought and action that must have a positive content. For example, if the Paris Commune was an event, it was because it demonstrated for the first time in world history that political power could belong to the workers and the poor, rather than to the propertied classes. And the 1917 Russian Revolution was an event because it demonstrated, for the first time in modern history, that a popular workers' insurrection in a large country could emerge victorious.

It is clear that from the late 1980s on, throughout the world there was a worldwide phenomenon of negation and destruction. A whole economic and political system, vaguely known as 'communism', ceased to exist. But was this disappearance the occasion of a creation, a novelty, something that political thought and action can seize upon? Revolutionaries have long had a saying: 'No construction without destruction.' This is true enough. But construction is not necessarily invention. After all, one can build by copying existing models. The question then becomes: What has been built on the ruins of the system of the ex-communist countries? Was this construction a real historical event, or was it a negation, real enough, but not an invention with a universal status?

I can tell you straight away my own answer to this question. It is only my answer, and I offer it up for discussion in two points.

The first point is that the destruction of the system of popular democracies, or socialist states if you like, especially in Czechoslovakia and Poland, but also in East Germany, Hungary, and of course China, could have given rise to an invention, to a new economic, social, and political creation. Why name these five countries in particular? Because they had already lived through a prior historical experience of popular uprisings against the socialist state system, which in fact blocked any possibility of a real movement towards communism. This system had the merit of having broken with the private ownership of the means of production, but in a completely paradoxical way; it confused the original communism, whose strategic project was the decline of the state, with the construction of a centralised state stuck fast in its despotic form. East Germany in 1953, Hungary in 1956, China between 1966 and 1976, Czechoslovakia in 1968, and Poland in the early 1980s, all experienced episodes of insurrection against this kind of state. And in at least three cases – in Czechoslovakia with Dubček's socialist reformism, in China with the propositions of the Cultural Revolution opposed to the dictatorship of the Party, and in Poland with the Solidarność movement – we saw the emergence of new political projects, born from within the communist world of the time.

There was therefore a precedent in the recent historical past for the destruction of the oppressive system of popular democracies, to be followed by an invention that, under the reinvented name of 'communism', would have been something of interest to political thought in general.

The second point is that, alas (I would say), this did not happen. The system of popular democracies was replaced by other things well known to all of us, things far older than the popular democracies themselves: in the economic sphere, the liberal-style reign of capitalist private property; in the social sphere, the destruction of collective systems of protection for the poorest and the reappearance of very significant inequalities as a direct conse-quence of personal wealth and corruption; and, finally, in the political sphere, either electoral parliamentary democracy or openly oligarchic authoritarian forms.

Basically, the destruction did not give rise to a political invention at all, but to a kind of catch-up: the collective mode of organisation in the central European countries and in Russia is now the same one that existed in Western Europe at the end of the nineteenth century. As for China, under the direction of the bizarrely named 'communist' party, there we have a state monopoly capitalism, centralised and policed, akin to that which existed in 1850s France in the era of Napoleon III. At that time France had an electoral system of 'official candidates', a role played quite naturally in China by the officials of the one existing party.

The interesting question then becomes: What possibilities were available for maintaining the vitality of the communist idea? And why did choice or historical necessity lead the socialisms of the twentieth century, after the fiasco, towards pure and simple integration into globalised capitalism in its pre-established Western form or in even more archaic forms?

In addressing this issue we will use the diagram below.

Contemporary Structure

MODERNITY

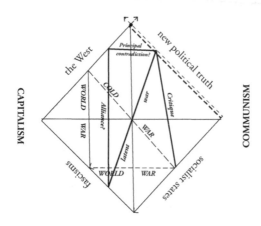

TRADITION

The aim here is to analyse, in a general context, the historical and subjective conditions in which the popular democracies came to an end – the end of what once presented themselves as socialist states.

The fundamental assumption of this diagram is that the principal subjective effects of the contemporary world situation since the 1980s cannot be understood on the basis of just a single contradiction. Today, in fact, the types of political propaganda available are three in number:

(1) The propaganda of the Western imperial camp – of the zones, countries, or states in which the great globalised system of capitalism in its most advanced form dominates – presents these zones as the sole representative of the only possible political modernity: the democratic representative state that derives its legitimacy from free elections. The main contradiction, against the backdrop of capitalism considered as natural, self-evident, and irreplaceable, is the contradiction between dictatorship and democracy, or between despotism and the republic, so this propaganda tells us. Which, by the way, brings us back almost verbatim to the political debates of the late eighteenth century, debates far older and more well worn than those surrounding the communist hypothesis. In light of this, let us dare to say that communism is still not an archaism, and will not be so for a long time to come, but is in fact the youth of the world. So much for the first mode of propaganda, the one that dominates in our own country.

(2) Without contesting globalised capitalism in the slightest, another camp, which I call reactive, appeals to tradition in opposition to

modernity. Often this reactive camp lays claim to some ethnic or religious identity. It may be Christianity, as in the right wing of the Republican Party in the United States, or Islam, as in Turkey and Iran and among the armed gangs that are ravaging the Middle East and parts of Africa. It may be Jewish singularity, as in Israel, or a renewed militaristic nationalism, as in Japan, India, Hungary, or Putin's Russia. All of these may define local particularities. But the main point is that, without exception, all of these movements affirm the compatibility between a traditional reactive appeal to roots and mainstream capitalism. So we can call this mode of propaganda 'fascism'. For what is the broadest definition of fascism? We might say that fascism is a dogged antimodernist vision of the world, nostalgic for the era of nations, religions, and conservatism, but that it remains violently articulated with capitalism itself. The principal contradiction for this current is, against the background of capitalism as natural and self-evident, the contradiction between the vices of modern freedom and the traditional order, between societal democratism and the cult of some identity or other.

(3) Finally, there is a militant camp, now rather weakened on the global scale, which maintains that the principal contradiction is still that opposing a movement of collective emancipation and, as Marx said, of free association, going by the name of communism, to capitalism itself.

In short, three contradictions that are declared officially by states, by public opinion, or by certain small groups to be the principal contradiction: two are set against a presumed background of capitalism: the contradiction between dictatorship and democracy and the contradiction between modernity and tradition. The other is a direct attack on the dominant capitalism, and affirms that the principal contradiction, for two centuries, has been and remains that between capitalism and private property and communism and free collective association.

The latter orientation is my own. But I propose to look at the current conjuncture from the point of view of two contradictions and not just one. My thesis is that events in the contemporary world clearly demonstrate that, in the consciousness of the masses, and particularly in that fraction known as the middle classes, or more accurately the educated petty bourgeoisie, *the contradiction between modernity and tradition ultimately operates against the contradiction between capitalism and emancipation. As a result, a division centred on the desire for the West as the only recourse against tradition exposes the movement as a whole to authoritarian capture in the service of the interests of globalised capitalism.*

Let's take a closer look at the diagram.

In it we can see the complex of the two intertwined contradictions of the contemporary world: the one that opposes modernity to the world of tradition, and the one that opposes capitalism to communism. At the centre, at the intersection of the two, there is the equivocation of contemporary subjectivities, pulled in all directions, so to speak, between four determinations: (1) The temptation to identify with traditions (in our case, 'being French', 'French values'); (2) fascination with modernity (for us, commodities, money, tourism, freedom of morals, etc.); (3) the dominant allegiance to capitalism (as the only possible way to organise societies); and (4) Communism (as an absolute value, both past and dreamed of for the future).

On the edge of the diagram, going counter-clockwise, we find first of all capitalism's monopoly on the desire for modernity. This dominant correlation between capitalism and modernity is what I call 'the West'. Next, you have the fact that, in spite of this correlation, there are many attempts to articulate capitalism with identities, with religious, national, familialist, or other motifs. Capitalism tolerates such attempts, but they are only viable if they are supported by despotic states. The ever-present connection between capitalism and various forms of reactive identities is what I call 'fascism'. And then there is the historical correlation between tradition and communism, embodied by the socialist states of the previous century. These states, and the communist parties that ruled them, largely guaranteed the stability of their non-capitalist power through a distrust of all modernity (except their own brand), and a sense of allegiance consolidated by all sorts of reactive themes, in the field of morals (open hostility to the legalisation of abortion and homosexuality), art ('socialist realism' as a cover for formal conservatism), the family (maintained and encouraged), and even national identity ('my Party has returned to me the colours of France', as Aragon wrote), and race (traces of anti-Semitism and a colonial contempt for dominated peoples).

And lastly, on the fourth side, indicated by a dotted line as a programme must be, we have the construction of a new communist politics, that of the current century, which would invent a new type of modernity capable of countering capitalist modernity and thus breaking with what today is the planetary force of the desire for the West. This is what we must work towards.

The diagram also shows various more diagonal connections across the square. It is clear for example that the Second World War was based on a tactical accord between the Western powers and the socialist states against the vast fascist project deployed in Europe by the Nazis and their allies. Similarly, the Cold War that followed was a confrontation between the Western powers and the socialist states, from which the West emerged victorious. In my opinion, this was because twentieth-century communism was unable to wrest politics from the archaism of the despotic state, and thus remained anchored to a traditional vision, unable to compete on a global scale with the desire for the West. It also indicates that, against the threat of a new communism, the West can always be tempted by an alliance with the fascisms against which it claims to struggle, but which it already tolerates all over the world today.

Finally, the diagram shows, this time quite rightly in bold, that the new communist politics is defined by a threefold task: to embody the pole that is contradictory with and antagonistic to Western capitalist modernity; to lead the conflict against fascisms; and to produce its own independent and innovative critical assessment of the experience of the socialist states, based in the first instance upon the lessons to be drawn from the Cultural Revolution in China.

We can see that the collapse of the socialist states and the abandonment of the communist idea opens up not just one but three possibilities:

(1) The reactionary tendency that revolves around the fixed point of tradition – nationalist traditions in politics, religious, or moral traditions in the regulation of private life, conservative and authoritarian traditions at the state level. The aim here is to reattach tradition to capitalism, and thus to put a new fascism on the agenda.

This is the path being followed by the Orbán government in Hungary, it exists as a permanent temptation in Poland and, behind the scenes, it is the current orientation in Putin's Russia. It is also a trend that is violently present across vast areas of Asia, the Middle East, and Africa, particularly in the Muslim space, where it is conditioned by religious ideology. And it is also the vision of the extreme right-wing groups proliferating in Western Europe, including the French *Rassemblement National*.

(2) The moderate conservative position, which identifies with the West in the name of securing the privileges of modernity. Measured criticism of tradition on the one hand, especially with regard to moral liberalism and political pluralism, against more authoritarian governments. Radical criticism of communism on the other hand, and thus unabashed integration into globalised capitalism and the sovereignty of private property. This is the dominant orientation in those countries loosely referred to as 'the West'.

(3) The invention of a new politics, this time revolving around the communist pole, in such a way as to connect that pole to modernity. This

would incorporate the lessons and the propositions, but also a thinking through of the limits, of everything that took place in the socialist countries, especially during the 1960s and 1970s. This path remains virtually unexplored to date.

The central reason for this is that modernity today is deeply articulated with capitalism, in the really dominating figure of the Western world, the United States and Europe in particular. As a result, its subjective force – what I call *the desire for the West* – prevails over all others, and does so throughout the world. When it is prevented from doing so, at least apparently so as in China or Russia or in the Middle East, it is only by falling back on traditional subjective formations such as nationalism or religion, which precisely have no universal status. And when it is violently opposed by fundamentalist religious groups, the result is the practice of mass murder as the sole instrument of propaganda, which presents the perfect opportunity for Western states to comfort themselves in the name of the combined values of the Republic and liberal capitalism.

Against this desire for the West, but also against the false negations of this desire, only a new idea can prevail, giving rise to a new desire. A strategic idea, which can be reduced to four points:

(1) It is possible to organise collective life around something other than private property and profit. Capitalism is not and must not be the end of history.

(2) It is possible to organise production around something other than specialisation and the division of labour. There is no reason why the separation between intellectual and manual labour, or between managerial and executive tasks, should remain in force. We must enter the era of what Marx called the polymorphous worker.

(3) It is possible to organise collective life without reference to identitarian closed sets such as nations, languages, religions, and customs. All of these differences can and must coexist in a fruitful way, but on the political scale of humanity as a whole. The future lies in a complete internationalism.

(4) It is possible to gradually dismantle the state as a separate power with a monopoly on violence. The free association of people, along with a shared rationality, can and must replace law and coercion.

These four points practically make up the definition of communism as we find it in Marx and other nineteenth-century thinkers. Only with the restoring of its force and its true meaning will the undermining of the seductive power of capitalist modernity commence.

It is therefore a question of bringing into existence the fourth side of the diagram: the one on the top right, which ought to have served consistently and forcefully to link communism to modernity, as it did in the nineteenth century, and again in Russia in the 1920s, and then in China in the 1960s, thus creating, against the reign of the market, a new modernity: a modernity outside of monetary circulation, profit, and the consumption of useless products, a creative and disinterested modernity. It is this modernity that must be made to exist in all particular mobilisations, in all collective actions and inventions, and on a global scale.

The four points also allow us to propose our own assessment of the failure of socialist states in the twentieth century.

In effect, the Soviet revolution dealt almost exclusively with the first of the four points of the Communist Idea. It broke with bourgeois property rights and placed production entirely in the hands of the state, for the first time in human history. But after Lenin's death, the Russian revolution practically stalled at this first point. This stage involving the state and the legal system, including the question of property, is necessary, but by no means sufficient. There must be a passage from state ownership to what has been called the property of the whole people, where the working community is also and at the same time master of the instruments of production. But under Stalin the state system was secured and protected in a terroristic manner, and the three other points of the communist programme were abandoned. Nationalism reappeared against internationalism, the division of labour was maintained and even aggravated, and the state, far from being called into question, was constantly reinforced.

In China, the Cultural Revolution addressed points (2) and (4). The question of labour and the organisation of labour, the relationship between workers and technicians or engineers, the difference between a socialist and a capitalist factory, all took centre stage in the discussions. A document like the one drafted by the workers of the Shanghai machine-tool factory remains an exceptional testimony to this. A new kind of medicine was promoted, which went to the sick poor in remote areas, the model proposed being that of 'barefoot doctors'. The question of the relationship between manual and intellectual work was tackled head-on. In particular, workers' groups for the study of philosophy appeared. On point (4), in the context of a gigantic, anarchic, and violent mass movement, the greatest possible freedom of popular movements was encouraged, including those against the dominant party: a political vision synthesised in Mao's text *The Sixteen Points*. There was an experiment with the introduction, as a new basis for the state, of committees bringing together and as far as possible uniting former Communist Party militants, young revolutionaries, and old-school state officials. This was called the 'Shanghai Commune', and was the first quite remarkable experiment to draw directly upon the lessons of the Paris Commune. This intermediate form between mass movement and state apparatus subsequently came to be called the 'Revolutionary Committee'. In short, the state itself was subjected to formal modifications introduced on the initiative of the mass movement.

None of this was preserved after Deng Xiao Ping's military coup. But it remains our historical and intellectual heritage, just like the inventions of the Paris Commune.

The new communism consists in the flexible mobilisation of these four fundamental points, their presence, their necessary introduction wherever there are popular movements or new forms of organisation. It consists in the invention of a tight dialectic between state forms and the forms of the mass movement, between power and revolt. The whole thing aims at the construction of a political modernity, but also a social, productive, working, intellectual, artistic, and technological modernity, capable of competing with the contemporary, inegalitarian, deadly militaristic monopoly of capitalist modernity.

I would like to conclude with a metaphor for this new modern breath of life that will bring about the inevitable resurrection of the communist strategy, by way of a poem with which many of you are probably already familiar, and which gives some idea of the style of this modernity, of its breath, of the hope that it conveys. It is Arthur Rimbaud's poem 'Genius', from the collection *Illuminations*. Wherever Rimbaud says 'he', meaning the genius, I invite you to hear, if only tonight, 'the new communism' – and I leave it to poetry to rally you to the cause!

Genius

Because he has opened the house to foaming winter and to noisy summer, he is affection, he is now, he who purified what we drink, what we eat, he who is the charm of brief visits and the unearthly delight of destinations. He is affection, he is the future, strength, and love that we, standing in furious boredom, watch, passing through tempestuous skies, flying flags of ecstasy.

He is love, reinvented in perfect measure, reason both marvelous and unforeseen, and eternity: an instrument adored for its fatality. We have all known the terror of his sacrifice and of our own: Let us delight in our health, in the vigor of our faculties, in selfish affection and passion for him who loves us throughout his infinite days ...

And we remember, and he embarks ... And if Adoration goes away, and nonetheless rings, his promise rings: 'Enough of these superstitions, these old bodies, these houses and days. Our time has fallen away!'

He will not depart, he will not descend from a heaven once again, he will not manage to redeem women's anger, and men's laughter, and all our sin: for it is already done, by his being, and being loved.

O his breaths, his faces, his flights; the terrible speed of formal perfection and action.

O fertile mind, boundless universe!

His body! Long-dreamt release and shattering grace meet new violence!

The sight of him, his sight! All old genuflections and sorrows are *lifted* in his wake.

His day! The abolition of all streaming, echoing sufferings through a music more intense.

His stride! Migration is more momentous than ancient invasions.

O he, and we! Old charities pale before such benevolent pride.

O world! And the clear song of new sorrows!

He knew us all and loved us all. This winter night, from cape to cape, from farthest pole to nearest chateau, from crowd to beach, from face to face, with weary emotions and waning strength, let us hail him, and see him, and send him forth, and down beneath the tides and up in snowy deserts, let us seek this sight, his breath, his body, his day.[1]

Three points on this extraordinary text:

(1) Rimbaud attributes to the Genius – and we will therefore attribute to the new communism – two contradictory attributes: he is, we are told, both the 'charm of brief visits' and 'the unearthly delight of destinations'. This indeed is how we must identify the fulcrums of new communism and its work, both local and global: it comes forth in almost elusive singularities, but it also proceeds towards the most solidly established construction. And it is important that we should never sacrifice one to the other, neither the nomadism of elusive places to the immobility of powers, nor the necessity of a shared strategic vision to the opportunism of circumstances.

(2) Rimbaud also tells us that politics, true politics, must ensure a real exit from the dominant world. It must organise the exit from capitalism just as, for Plato, philosophy ensures the exit

[1] Arthur Rimbaud, 'Genius', in *A Season in Hell and Illuminations*, tr. Wyatt Mason (New York: Modern Library, 2005).

from the Cave of the merely apparent. This is what he calls the 'long-dreamt release'. And once again, this exit implies two things: the positive reception of the event, of that which authorises the hope of a radical novelty by breaking the laws of domination. This is what Rimbaud calls 'shattering grace'. And then active invention, the work towards the most distant consequences of this event, those that will destroy the old order – or what Rimbaud calls 'new violence'.

(3) And, finally, he tells us that this political novelty must be desired, affirmed and called forth, but that we must also seek it out, discover where lies the path that our political thinking must take. Moreover, we must also talk about it to others, relay it to others, with the requisite enthusiasm. This new element in which communism is built, we must, Rimbaud tells us, 'Hail it, and see it, and send it forth'.

These will be my last words. May we all know how to see and to hail the coming communism and send it forth, renewed, to this whole world from which, at the moment, it is sorely lacking.

Part II

Thinking the Present from the To-Come

5

Lessons From the 'Gilets Jaunes' Movement

What should we think – I mean thinking, not running around barking – about the violent, enduring contradiction between the 'gilet jaunes' movement and the state authorities, led by our little President Macron?

I said firmly, as soon as the final round of the presidential election was over, that I would never rally to either Marine Le Pen, captain of the parliamentary extreme Right, or to Macron, who was mounting what I called 'a democratic coup d'état' in the pseudo-reformative service of big capital.

Obviously, I have not changed my judgement on Macron. I despise him unreservedly. But what about the gilets jaunes movement? I must admit that, at least during its early days last year, I found nothing in its composition, its statements or its practices that seemed *politically* innovative or progressive to my eyes.

I agree unhesitatingly that the reasons for this revolt are numerous, and that, as such, the movement can be considered legitimate. I know about the desertification of rural areas, the sad silence of the abandoned streets in small and even medium-sized towns; the continual withdrawal of public services for masses of people, public services which anyway are gradually being privatised: pharmacies, hospitals, schools, post offices, railway stations, telephone networks. I know that pauperisation, at first creeping and then accelerating, is affecting populations that as recently as forty years ago were enjoying an almost continuous increase in spending power. Certainly, new forms of taxation and rises in taxation may seem to be one cause of this impoverishment. I am well aware that the material life of entire families is becoming a headache, particularly for many women, who indeed are very active in the gilets jaunes movement.

To sum up: there is great discontent in France among what may be called the working, mostly provincial, and moderate-income echelon of the middle class. The gilets jaunes movement is a significant expression of this discontent, in the form of an active and virulent revolt.

The historical and economic reasons for this uprising are perfectly clear for those who want to hear them. They also explain why the gilets jaunes place the beginning of their misfortunes forty years ago – roughly speaking in the 1980s, with the beginning of a long capitalist-oligarchic counter-revolution, wrongly known as 'neo-liberal' when it was just liberal tout court. That is, it was a return to the savagery of nineteenth-century capitalism. This counter-revolution was a reaction to the 'red years' – roughly from 1965 to 1975 – of which the epicentre in France was May '68, and the world epicentre the Cultural Revolution in China. But it was considerably accelerated by the collapse of the planetary enterprise of communism, in the USSR and then in China: nothing, on a global scale, any longer stood in the way of capitalism and its profiteers, and more specifically the exercise of unlimited power by a transnational billionaire oligarchy.

Of course, the French bourgeoisie joined with the counter-revolutionary movement. Indeed, they were its intellectual and ideological focal point, along with the activities of the 'nouveaux philosophes' who ensured that the communist Idea was hunted down everywhere not only as false, but as criminal. A number of intellectuals, turncoats from May '68 and Maoism, became conscientious watchdogs, under the auspices of inoffensive fetish-words of the bourgeois liberal counter-revolution including 'freedom', 'democracy', and 'our republic'.

However, the situation in France has gradually deteriorated from the 1980s to the present day. The country is no longer what it was during the 'Trente Glorieuses', the years of post-war reconstruction. France is no longer a major world power, a conquering empire. Today it is commonly compared with Italy and even Greece. Competition is pushing it out everywhere, and it can no longer count on its African colonial rent. Moreover, since the price of labour in Asia, for example, is far lower than in France, all of the big factories are gradually relocating abroad. This mass de-industrialisation is leading to a kind of social devastation that extends throughout whole regions, such as Lorraine with its steel industry and the North of France with its textile factories and coal mines, and into the suburbs of Paris, now given over to property speculation on the countless wastelands left behind by ruined industries.

The consequence of all of this is that the French bourgeoisie, the dominant oligarchy of the country, the shareholders of the CAC 40, can no longer maintain a politically subservient middle class in its service on the same footing as they did before, in particular before the 2008 crisis. This middle class had provided almost constant historical support for the electoral pre-eminence of the various right-wing parties, whose efforts were directed against the organised workers of the large industrial concentrations that had been tempted by communism between the 1920s and, precisely, the 1980s to 1990s. Hence the current uprising of a large popular part of this middle class that feels abandoned, an uprising against Macron, the local agent of capitalist 'modernisation', meaning a tightening of screws everywhere, savings, the introduction of austerity, and privatisation, all without the same consideration for the comfort of the middle classes that was afforded thirty years ago in exchange for their consent to the dominant system.

The gilets jaunes, pointing to their very real impoverishment, want to be properly paid for this consent again, and at full price. But this is absurd, since Macronism is precisely a consequence of the fact that, first of all, since the communist threat disappeared, the oligarchy has had less need of middle-class support, which was always costly to buy in; and secondly, that it can no longer afford to pay for electoral servitude on the same scale as in the past. And that it is therefore necessary, under the guise of 'indispensable reforms', to move towards a more authoritarian politics: a new form of state power will serve to enforce a lucrative 'austerity' extending from the unemployed and the workers to the lower strata of the middle class. All of this for the benefit of the real masters of the world, namely the principal shareholders in the large companies in industry, trade, raw materials, transport and communications.

In the *Communist Party Manifesto*, written in 1848, Marx already examined this type of conjuncture, and spoke with precision about what we see in the gilets jaunes today. He wrote that

[t]he lower middle class, the small manufacturer, the shopkeeper, the artisan, the peasant, all these fight

against the bourgeoisie, to save from extinction their existence as fractions of the middle class. They are therefore not revolutionary, but conservative. Nay more, they are reactionary, for they try to roll back the wheel of history.

They are trying to roll it back today all the more determinedly in so far as, given the turn taken by globalised capitalism, the French bourgeoisie is no longer in a position to maintain, let alone increase, their purchasing power. The gilets jaunes are indeed 'fighting against the bourgeoisie', as Marx put it, quite so. But they are fighting in the hope of restoring an old and outdated order, not inventing the new one whose name was and remains 'communism'. For everything that is not in one way or another moving in the direction of communism remains capitalist. In politics there are only two paths.

Let us then return to the concrete characteristics of the gilets jaunes movement. Its spontaneous characteristics, so to speak, those that do not owe to interventions from outside the mainstream of the uprising, are in fact 'reactionary', as Marx put it, but in a more modern sense: we might call the subjectivity of this movement a popular individualism, into which is condensed all the personal anger felt at the new forms of servitude that the dictatorship of Capital now imposes upon us all.

This is why it is wrong to say, as some do, that the gilets jaunes movement is intrinsically fascist. No. Fascism generally makes use of identitarian, national, or racial motifs in a very disciplined, even militarised way. In these protests, disorganised as the urban middle class always is, even verging on the individualistic, there are people of all kinds, from all walks of life, who often sincerely think of themselves as democrats, and who call upon the laws of the Republic, which, in today's France, is hardly going to help. In fact, any properly political convictions the vast majority of them may have are inconstant at best. Considering this movement, once again in its initial 'purity', from the point of view of its rare collective aspects, its slogans, its repeated statements, I don't see anything that speaks to me, interests me, gets me excited. Their proclamations, their perilous lack of organisation, the forms of action they pursue, their apparent absence of general thinking and strategic vision, all of this makes political inventiveness impossible. Moreover, I am not impressed by their hostility to any embodied leadership, their obsessive fear of centralisation and of the unified collective, a fear that, as with all contemporary reactionary formations, results from a confusion of democracy with individualism. None of this is likely to stand much of a chance as an enduring progressive, innovative, and victorious force against the miserable, odious Macron.

I know that right-wing opponents of the movement, especially those turncoat intellectuals, those ex-revolutionaries who became apologists for police power as soon as the oligarchy and the state provided them with platforms for their liberal chatter, accuse the gilets jaunes uprising of anti-Semitism or homophobia, or of 'endangering our Republic'. But I also know that, although there are indeed traces of all this in the movement, they are the result not of a shared conviction, but of a presence, an active infiltration, of the extreme Right into a movement that is disorganised to the point where it becomes prone to all manner of manipulations. But let's face it: various signs, including clear traces of short-sighted nationalism, latent hostility to intellectuals, demagogic 'democratism' in crypto-fascist 'people against the elites' style, and confusion in discourse, should make anyone wary of venturing an overall assessment of what exactly is afoot here. Let us at least agree that, since for the majority of gilets jaunes the gossip of 'social networks' takes the place of objective information, aberrant conspiracy theories are circulating throughout the movement.

There is an old saying, 'Not everything that moves is red'. And for the time being, although the gilet jaunes movement is certainly 'on the move', there is no 'red' in it; all I see, apart from the yellow, is the tricolour, which is always a little suspect in my eyes.

Of course, the ultra-leftists, the antifas, the waking sleepers of Nuit Debout, those who are always on the lookout for a 'movement' to get into, those who vaunt the 'coming insurrection', all celebrate democratic (in fact individualistic and short-sighted) proclamations, introduce the cult of decentralised assemblies, and imagine that they will soon be re-enacting the storming of the Bastille. But this jolly carnival cannot impress me: everywhere, for ten years and more, it has led to terrible defeats, paid for dearly by the people. Indeed, the 'movements' that made up the most recent historical sequence – from Egypt and the 'Arab Spring' to Occupy Wall Street, from the latter to the public squares of Turkey, from there to the riots in Greece, from Greece to *indignados* of all stripes, from *indignados* to Nuit Debout, from Nuit Debout to the gilets jaunes, and many others besides – seem quite ignorant of the real implacable laws that govern the world today. After the exhilarating movements and rallies, after occupations of all sorts, they are surprised that the game is so hard, and that one always fails, and even helps consolidate the opponent along the way. But the truth is that they have not even succeeded in constituting the beginnings of a real antagonism, of another way than contemporary capitalism, one universal in its scope.

Nothing is more important, in the present moment, than to keep in mind the lessons of this sequence of 'movements', including the gilets jaunes. They can be summarised as follows: *A movement whose unity is strictly negative will either fail, most often resulting in a situation worse than the one that prevailed over its origin, or it will have to split in two, beginning with the creative emergence from within it of an affirmative political proposition that is truly antagonistic to the dominant order, a proposition supported by disciplined organisation.*

All movements in recent years, regardless of location and duration, have followed almost the exact same catastrophic trajectory:

– an initial unity constituted strictly against the sitting government: this is the moment that may be called 'dégagiste', from '*Mubarak dégage*' to '*faire la fête à Macron*';

– a unity ensured by a complementary slogan, which is itself exclusively negative, after a period of anarchic brawls; when duration begins to weigh heavy on mass action, a slogan like 'down with repression', 'down with police violence': for lack of real political content, the 'movement' ceases to make any claims beyond the wounds inflicted on it;

– a unity defeated by electoral procedure, when one part of the movement decides to participate, another not, without any real political content behind either the positive or the negative response: as I write these lines, the electoral forecast places Macron back at pre-gilets-jaunes levels, the Right and far Right combined claiming more than 60 per cent and the only hope of the defunct Left, France Insoumise, at only seven per cent.

The consequence then is the rise to power, through elections, of something even worse than before. Either the coalition already in place wins, with a crushing victory (as was the case in May '68 in France); or a 'new' formula, which in fact is alien to the movement and very unpleasant, proves victorious (in Egypt, the Muslim Brotherhood, then the army with Al-Sissi; in Turkey, Erdogan); or the self-declared leftists are elected, but immediately capitulate on the content of their demands (Syriza in Greece); or the far Right alone is victorious (the case of Trump in the United States); or a group from the movement joins forces with the far Right to install itself in government (the Italian case, with the alliance of the Five Star Movement and the fascistoids of the Northern League). Let us note that this last possibility has some chance of coming to pass in France, if a functional alliance can be forged between an organisation that has supposedly emerged from the gilets jaunes and Marine Le Pen's electoral faction.

All of this because a negative unity is incapable of proposing a politics, and therefore will end up being crushed in whatever struggle it joins. But in order to propose a beyond of negation, it is necessary first to identify the enemy and to know what it means to really do something different from them, something absolutely other. This implies, *at the very least*, an effective knowledge of contemporary capitalism on a global scale, of the decadent place that France occupies within it, of communist-type solutions concerning property, the family (inheritance) and the state, and of the immediate measures that must be taken to set these solutions in motion, along with an agreement, based on a review of historical data, on the forms of organisation appropriate to achieve these imperatives.

Only a communist organisation resurrected on new bases can take on all of this by rallying to the future, as it were, a certain proportion of the routed middle classes. It is then possible, as Marx writes, that the middle classes will become 'revolutionary [...] in view of their impending transfer into the proletariat; they thus defend not their present, but their future interests, they desert their own standpoint to place themselves at that of the proletariat'.

These words of Marx's give us a valuable indication, authorising an only partially positive conclusion, but on an essential point: there is undoubtedly a potential Left in the gilets jaunes movement, a very interesting minority made up of those activists in the movement who are discovering that their cause must be thought of in the future tense and not the present, and who, in the name of this future, are devising ways to rally to something other than static demands on purchasing power, taxes, or the parliamentary reform.

We might then say that this minority can form part of a real people, the people in the sense that it is the bearer of a stable political conviction embodying a path truly antagonistic to the liberal counter-revolution.

Of course, without the incorporation en masse of new proletarians, the gilets jaunes cannot represent 'the people' as such. That would be to reduce this people to the most deprived section of the middle class, and their nostalgia for their bygone social status. To form a political people today, the mobilised mass must include a strong and visible contingent of the nomadic proletariat of our suburbs, a proletariat come from Africa, Asia, Eastern Europe, and Latin America; it must show clear signs of breaking with the dominant order. First of all in its visible signs – the red flag instead of the tricolour. And then in what it says, in leaflets and banners with directives and declarations antagonistic to that order. And, even further, in the demands it should be making – at a minimum, a total halt to privatisation and the cancellation of all privatisations that have taken place since the mid-1980s. The principal idea must be collective control over all of the means of production, the entire banking system, and all public services (health, education, transport, communication). In short, if they are to exist, the political people cannot be satisfied with bringing together a few thousand malcontents, or even a hundred thousand, I would say, and begging the State – rightly declared to be detestable – to 'listen' to them, organise referendums for them (on what?), provide a few more local services, or increase their spending power a little by reducing taxes.

Beyond the hyperbole and bluster, the gilets jaunes movement may very well prove useful in future. For, if we turn to that minority of activists in the movement who, by dint of meeting, acting, and speaking out, have understood in a sort of intuitive way that they need to acquire an overall vision of the true source of their misfortune on a global as well as a national scale – namely, the liberal counter-revolution – and who in consequence are ready to participate in the successive steps towards the construction of a new type of communist force, these gilets jaunes, thinking from their future, will undoubtedly contribute to the existence, here and now, of a political people. This is why we must talk with them and, if they agree, organise meetings with them in which we can construct the first principles of the new communism.

To begin with, these new activists will provide support for something I hold to be indispensable: creating, wherever possible, from the great suburbs to the small deserted towns, schools where the laws of capital and what it means to fight them in the name of a totally different political orientation are taught and discussed with clarity. If, beyond the episode of 'yellow vests versus white Macron', on the strength of the best that this episode has to offer for the future, a network of such red political schools could be created, then the movement, through its indirect power to awaken, would have proved to have been of true importance.

6

Pandemic, Ignorance, and New Sites of Collectivity

The current pandemic is by no means an exceptional or unprecedented event. There have been many serious epidemics in recent decades. The HIV (AIDS) epidemic killed millions of people around the world. The Hong Kong flu, in the winter of 1969–70, killed 32,000 people in France in two months, yet attracted little attention. We have every reason to believe that the death toll today will be far lower than that of malaria or AIDS, or even the combined total of successive influenza outbreaks.

The real difference between the present situation and the past is therefore not related to its cause, its natural real, the Sars-2 virus, the pandemic. It concerns the attention of states, the media and public opinion, which has been far more heavily mobilised than in those past instances. And this is because the 'big' countries, the so-called 'democracies', are severely affected. An equally important point is that, in the absence of any vaccine (at least during the first year of the epidemic) and any remedy, the only means of protection is containment, which presupposes a discipline that our liberal individualistic societies are neither accustomed to nor inclined to adopt.

What are states to do? Faced with an exceptional situation, whether a war or a pandemic, bourgeois states (and unfortunately, that is the only type in existence today) are forced to take measures that go beyond their strict class-based logic. The hospital system has to function as well as possible, hotel rooms have to be requisitioned to confine the sick, the movement of people carrying the virus across borders has to be limited, and so on. But throughout all of this, states must also protect the future of the structure of society as a whole, namely its class-based nature. Governing becomes a more difficult exercise than in more normal circumstances. Fortunately for existing states, the real enemy of the types of society we live in, which is not the virus but communism, is so enfeebled today that they are sure to get by without too much trouble, at least in the short term.

Public reaction to placatory speeches on the return of 'happy days' will not bring them down. The parliamentary regime, which is the natural political regime of developed capitalism, and which in France is still praised under the twofold fetish-name of 'democracy' and 'our Republic', has seen worse! If Macron has to be removed, then the masters of the game will do it themselves, to the applause of all kinds of malcontents who, for two years, have seen the bland Macron as the cause of all our ills, when, in fact, as has been the case for the past two centuries, our ills stem from the coupling, particularly tight at the present moment, between private property (which can be praised and promised to all) and the 'iron law' of the concentration of capital (which ensures that private property benefits only the very few).

We then hear, and this time for solid reasons, talk of an inevitable economic crisis. But 'economic crises' are inherent to capitalism itself; we might say that it belongs to the essence of capitalism to lurch from crisis to crisis. The last one was in 2008. What have we seen since then in the various 'movements'? A consensual refusal of the word 'communism'; the inability to centre and unify their actions under the crucial slogan 'no to privatisation, present and past'; an obsessional focus on the personnel of government, who are always, as Marx already noted, made up of perfectly interchangeable 'middle-managers of Capital'. Under these conditions, the crisis (or crises) do not seem to have put the slightest dent in the self-evidence of capitalism, its 'there is no alternative' aspect. What to me seems perilous in this conjuncture, what seems to favour all forms of reaction, is the ignorance of these obvious facts and the scant credit given to conclusive reasoning and scientifically established observations. The real sciences are one of the few areas of human endeavour that deserves trust, one of the principal common treasures of humanity, from mathematics to biology via physics and chemistry, along with the Marxist study of society and politics, not to forget psychoanalysis's discoveries in relation to disorders of subjectivity. The real problem is that trust in rationality is very often ignorant and blind, and that, as we see today, many people, perhaps the majority, have come to trust in false sciences, absurd miracles, old hat and impostors. This makes the situation entirely obscure and brings about inconsistent prophecies about 'the day after'. Mao was quite right when he said that 'without the ideological preparation of opinion, no political action is possible'.

At the heart of the assessment of the pandemic crisis, and of all 'crises', should therefore be the constitution, by all willing activists, of a vast network of schools where everything that needs to be known in order to live and act in our societies could be taught to all who wish to learn.

In this respect the École des Actes, created in Aubervilliers with the support of the Théâtre de la Commune, is in my opinion an example that ought to be followed in all metropolitan suburbs. Here one can learn simultaneously from the experiences and questions of the popular public, with at its heart the nomadic proletarians (those misnamed 'migrants') everything that, in the diverse forms of rationality, is necessary to survive, to speak, to read, to think.

These schools will also organise – the École des Actes is doing this right now – material and administrative help for those who need it, with a canteen for hot meals, a dispensary for first aid, serious thinking on housing, and counsellors to secure people's rights, both those that exist and those that should exist in virtue of the laws of people's lives. And no doubt many other things yet to be devised.

As soon as public meetings are allowed, every week or, in case of a major problem, the School will hold a general assembly, where anyone who has something to say or a question to ask, or a criticism, or a new proposal, will be able to speak. Interventions will be translated into all languages spoken in the School. At the École des Actes, for example, at the moment translations are made into English (for those from Bangladesh), Soninke, Fulani, and Arabic. Until large meetings are possible again, an online newspaper, food collections and distributions, and small but regular meetings will ensure that the school remains running.

A federation of schools based on this model will, I believe, be an important step towards the emergence of a new political programme. Here, together with the people concerned, we can reflect upon a way for humanity to finally emerge from its self-imprisonment in the world of class societies. It will be a question of putting an end to the interminable Neolithic sequence that has been our lot for four or five thousand years now, under the yoke of the unbreakable triptych of private property, family, and state.

If, by chance, a wider discussion should open up concerning this kind of proposition, then there will be a chance that the pandemic will have not been at once biologically mortifying, intellectually impoverishing, and politically sterile.

7

Movements Without an Idea and an Idea for Movements

A rational political assessment of the current situation has become a true rarity. Between the catastrophic preaching of the unintentionally religious contingent of ecology (we are approaching the Last Judgement) and the phantasmagorias of a disorientated Left (we are the contemporaries of exemplary 'struggles', irresistible 'mass movements', and the 'collapse' of liberal capitalism in crisis), it is difficult to locate any rational orientation, and a kind of mental chaos, whether militant or disenchanted, is setting in on all sides. Here I would like to introduce a few considerations, both empirical and prescriptive.

On a near global scale, for quite a few years now, since what was called the 'Arab Spring', we have been living in a world in which many struggles, or more precisely mass mobilisations and gatherings, are underway. I would say that the general conjuncture is marked, subjectively, by what I would call 'movementism' – that is, the widely shared belief that large popular gatherings will undoubtedly succeed in changing the situation. We see this from Hong Kong to Algiers, from Iran to France, from Egypt to California, from Mali to Brazil, from India to Poland, and in many other places and countries.

All of these movements, without exception, seem to me to have three characteristics:

(1) They are composite in their social origin, in the pretexts for their revolt, and in their spontaneous political convictions. This multiform aspect also clarifies why they are so numerous. They are not workers' groups or student movement demonstrations, or revolts of shopkeepers crushed by taxes, or feminist protests, or ecological prophecies, or regional or national dissidences, or the protests of those known as migrants but whom I call nomadic proletarians. They are a bit of everything, held together under the purely tactical domination of

one or several dominant tendencies, depending on place and circumstance.

(2) Given this situation it follows that, with the present state of ideologies and organisations, the unity of these movements is, and can only be, strictly negative. This negation of course stems from disparate realities. One can revolt against the action of the Chinese government in Hong Kong, against the appropriation of power by military cliques in Algiers, against the stranglehold of the religious hierarchy in Iran, against personal despotism in Egypt, against nationalist and racial reaction in California, against the action of the French army in Mali, against neo-fascism in Brazil, against the persecution of Muslims in India, against the retrograde stigmatisation of abortion and unconventional sexualities in Poland, and so on. But there is nothing else in these movements, and in particular nothing that would constitute a general counter-proposal. In the end, in the absence of a common political proposition that is clearly free of the constraints of contemporary capitalism, the movement ends up exercising its negative unity against a specific name, usually that of a head of state. Cries of '*Mubarak dégage*', 'Bolsonaro, fascist, out',

'Modi, racist, out', 'Trump out', 'Bouteflika retire'. Not forgetting, of course, the invective, the call for resignations and the personal stigma-tisation of our natural targets, which in France means none other than little Macron. I would say that all of these movements, all of these struggles, are most definitely 'dégagisms'. They want the current leader to leave but have not the slightest idea about either who will replace him, or the procedure by which, assuming that he does indeed leave, we can be sure that the situation will change. In short, negation, which unifies, carries with it no affirmation, no creative will, no active conception of the analysis of situations, or of what a new type of politics could or should be. In the absence of all this, we end up – and this signals the end of the movement – with an ultimate form of its unity, which is to define itself against the police repression of which it has been a victim, against the police violence that it has had to face. In short, the negation of its negation by the authorities. I had already experienced this in May '68, when, for lack of common affirmations, at least at the beginning of the movement, people shouted in the streets 'CRS, SS!' Fortunately, there were more interesting things to follow, once the primacy of this rebellious negativity had passed but at the price, of course, of a confrontation between opposing political conceptions, between different demands.

(3) Today, in the long term, the whole global movement is leading only to the strengthening of established power or to purely cosmetic change, which may turn out worse than what was being revolted against. Mubarak is gone, but Al-Sissi, who has replaced him, only represents another, perhaps worse, version of military power. China's grip on Hong Kong has ultimately strengthened, with laws more like those in Beijing and mass arrests of rebels. The religious camarilla in Iran remains intact. The most active reactionaries, such as Modi, Bolsonaro, and the Polish clerical clique, are doing just fine, thank you. And little Macron, enjoying a 43 per cent popularity rating in the polls, is not only in far better electoral health today than at the beginning of the struggles and movements, but has reached a level even better than his predecessors, who, whether the very reactionary Sarkozy or the very socialist Hollande, at the end of the same period of their mandate, were trailing at around 20 per cent positive opinion.

A historical comparison comes to mind here. In the years between 1847 and 1850, across a large part of Europe, great workers' and students' movements emerged: great mass uprisings against the despotic order that had been established since the Restoration of 1815 and had been subtly consolidated after the July Revolution in 1830. In the absence of a firm idea of what the representation of an essentially different politics could be, beyond a fulminating negation, the effervescence of the revolutions of 1848 only served to open up a new regressive sequence. In France, in particular, the result of this was the interminable reign of a typical exponent of nascent capitalism, Napoleon III, alias (in Victor Hugo's words) *Napoleon le Petit*.

However, in 1848, Marx and Engels, who had taken part in the uprisings in Germany, drew the lessons of the whole affair, both in texts of historical analysis such as the pamphlet entitled *Class Struggles in France*, and in that great manual in which they finally put forward an affirmative line, describing as it were for all time what an entirely new politics should be – the *Communist Party Manifesto*. It is around this affirmative construction, the 'manifesto' of a party which does not exist, but which *must* exist, that another history of politics begins. Marx would repeat the gesture twenty-three years later, drawing the lessons of an admirable attempt, which once again, beyond its heroic defence, lacked any effective organisation of its affirmative unity, namely the Paris Commune.

Of course, our circumstances are different! But I believe that everything today revolves around the need to subordinate negative slogans and defensive actions to a clear and synthetic vision of our own objectives. And I am convinced that to achieve this, we must by all means remind ourselves of the words that Marx declared to be a summary of his entire thought. This summary is also negative, but on such a scale that it can only be supported by a grandiose statement. It is the slogan 'abolition of private property'.

On closer inspection, slogans such as 'Defend our liberties' or 'Against police violence' are strictly conservative. The former implies that we have real freedoms to defend within the established order, when our central problem should be that, without equality, freedom is only a delusion. How can the nomadic proletarian without legal papers, whose entry into our country is a cruel saga, call himself 'free' in the same sense as the billionaire with real power, owner of a private plane and its pilot, hidden behind the electoral shop-window of his state middle-manager? And, if one is a consistent revolutionary, if one has an affirmative and rational desire for a world other than the one being contested, how could one imagine that the police that serve the powers that be can always be friendly, courteous and peaceful? That they could say to the rebels, some of whom are hooded and armed: 'The Elysée? Over there on the right, the one with the big gate?'

Better return to the heart of the matter: property. The unifying strategic slogan can immediately be, affirmatively: 'collectivisation of the entire process of production'. Its intermediate negative correlate, with immediate effect: 'abolition of all privatisations carried out by the state since 1986'. As for a good, purely tactical slogan to motivate those dominated by the desire for negation, it could be as follows: we move into the premises of an important department of the Ministry of the Economy and Finance, the *Commission des participations et des transferts*. We do it knowing that this esoteric name, *'participations et transferts'*, is only a transparent mask for the commission for privatisation created in 1986. And let us make it known that we will remain in this commission until the disappearance of all forms of private ownership of those things that are, in one way or another, a common good.

In just popularising these objectives, as strategic as they are tactical, believe me, we would open up a new era, after that of 'struggles', 'movements', and 'protests', whose negative dialectic is wearing thin, and wearing us out. We would be the pioneers of a new mass communism, whose 'spectre', as Marx said, would come back to haunt not only France or Europe, but the whole world.

8

World, Existence, Foreignness: A New Dawn for Politics

Does it not seem elementary and obvious, in politics, in light of the class struggle and the young Marx's definition of the new political subject, to declare that an existence – the existence of the nomadic proletarian, for example – that is occluded, denied, and repressed must, on the contrary, be affirmed and organised against the bourgeois order? Certainly. But any such declaration of existence takes up a position, in the last instance, in regard to the world. The class struggle only becomes organised thought in so far as it takes up a position in regard to the contemporary world. Lenin reminded us that the 'tasks' before us are only decidable if we are able to declare what 'the current situation' is.

And the situation is always the situation of the world.

But what exactly does it mean to make a statement about the world, especially today? I will take an example that is quite abstract and banal, but that many contemporary circumstances bring to the fore. Let us ask ourselves in what sense a religion, Christianity or Islam for example, inscribes its declarations of existence within the horizon of the world. Well, *religion essentially always declares that there are two worlds.* In religions, existence, as a category of thought, is entirely determined by variations of intensity that relate to the existence of two distinct worlds. Whether we call this duality 'sensible' versus 'supra-sensible', 'world of the finite' versus 'world of the infinite', or 'world of mortal finitude' versus 'world of paradise', there are in any case two worlds. One might even ask whether we ought not to count as 'religious' any evaluation of existence that asserts the prior existence of two worlds.

The consequences of this choice are manifold. For example, if there are two worlds then one can assert one's existence by dying. That's why the figure of the martyr has always been a major figure of religious apologia. It consists simply in saying, 'I can assert my existence by dying, because there are two worlds, and I die in one only to enter into the other.' Without this prior assumption, such acts are obviously utterly senseless.

Where do we stand in relation to assertions about the world today? This is all the more important because, as you know, much traditional state or political discourse consists in explaining to us that any assertion of existence can only be made relative to the world, i.e. that the constraints of the world are such that assertions of existence are themselves constrained. It is therefore of interest to interrogate the current state of the question regarding the relationship between assertions of existence and propositions about the world.

As you know, contemporary capitalism prides itself on being global. For a while, the fact that it is global was an object of critique: this was the case when Marx developed the theory of the world market, because the critique of political economy emphasised market globalisation as a new and unique feature. Today, on the contrary, the 'global' nature of capitalism is touted as being in itself the accomplishment of its destiny, and talk of 'globalisation' is everywhere. The thesis about the world is that there is an objective process of globalisation of the situation. As you know, the enemies of this globalisation say that they want 'another world'. They call for an 'alter-globalisation'. This proves that the world today is not only the place where bodies, discourses, truths, and subjects exist; the world is also what is at stake in the ideological-political battle.

But which world? That is the question, and it has always contained two different questions. An analytical or descriptive one – roughly speaking 'What kind of world do we live in?' or 'What is the world, what are worlds?' And then, after the description of worlds, the normative question 'What world do we want?', 'Precisely what kind of world do we want to declare that we exist in?' The link between these two questions, namely how to move from the world as it is to the world as we want it to be, can be seen as a basic definition of politics from the point of view of assertions about the world that govern or constitute the horizon of assertions of existence. So alterglobalisation, ecology, sustainable development, human rights, democracy – all of these practices define a politics in the sense that they answer the question: From within the world as it is, what is to be done in order to arrive at the world as we wish it to be?

Superficially, this seems very clear, so long as today we can say that *a* world exists. But can we? Personally, I don't think so. Today, at the scale we are looking at, from the point of view of the historical future of the human species, 'the' world does not exist. And the impoverished 'planet' of the ecological mystics cannot take its place. In active consciousness, in real experiences, in dominant politics, there are at least two worlds (e.g. the 'democratic' world and the 'totalitarian' world), and perhaps even more (e.g. nationalisms, each shut up in its own little world). Consequently, the dominant political question is not: How do we build the world we want, in and against the world we don't like? For that would presuppose that we share at least one thesis, the thesis of the possible unity of the desirable world. Neither the real world of capitalist globalisation nor the desirable world of realised communism nowadays assembles sufficient existential options to serve as the supports of a *single* world. The world is the horizon of questions of existence, but we are at the point where the amorphous dispersion of existential assertions calls into question the existence of the world itself. To me, the central contemporary question seems to be: How do we make *a* world exist? A world of living subjects, let's call it that. Because in reality such a world does not seem to exist. The world that exists, the world of globalisation, is, I would say, not a world of living subjects, a world of the plenitude of existence. It is only a world of objects and monetary signs, a world of the free circulation of products and flows. This world of the world market is ultimately just the world foreseen by Marx long ago: the world in which the value of existence takes as its norm the iciness of egoistical calculation.

In this world unified by a system of social classes, itself explicitly shaped on the pattern of objects and monetary signs, it seems highly unlikely that human subjects can exist freely and determine the unity of a desirable world. To begin with, the majority of human subjects have absolutely no basic right to move and settle wherever they want, in contrast to financial flows and commodities, which are – in principle, sometimes enforced by means of murderous wars

– subject to an international right to 'free trade'. The overwhelming majority of women and men in the so-called world, the world of products and signs, are unable to determine their existence on the basis of the supposed unity of this world. They are in no position to move through it, they are in no position to trace upon it the trajectory of their own existence. They cannot even effectively declare their existence within it, because they are mercilessly confined to what is in fact the *immanent outside* of this world.

What is the outside, in a world defined by objects and signs? Well, the outside designates those areas where there are precious few markets and where the circulation of money is, in general, the sole preserve of a handful of exploiters. If the world is defined by the circulation of objects and signs, then in places where objects become scarce or are even absent because they are sent elsewhere as commodities, in places where monetary signs travel only on skeletal private circuits, we find ourselves in the outside of the inside, since the identity of the world is defined by this circulation.

This principle of the enclosure of the outside of the world inside the world is something very concrete. As you know, today we find ourselves in the age of the building of walls. The 'Berlin Wall' came tumbling down, delivering East Germany to the world of objects and signs, with cries of 'Long live Western democracy'. But the truth is that, since then, walls have been built all over the world. This building of walls is a fundamental activity of the world itself: look at the wall that separates Palestinians and Israelis, the wall that separates Mexicans from Americans, or the electric fence that separates Africans from Spain. Not so long ago, the mayor of an Italian city, inspired by this state of affairs and wanting to affirm these worldly exigencies in his own way, proposed to build a wall between the city centre and the suburbs. Good idea, that way we can be sure that those awful 'suburban youths' will only burn their own cars! Ultimately, there are walls so that the poor, in particular nomadic proletarians, remain shut up in their homes, outside the world, even though it is supposedly *the* world. Those who are absolutely necessary to do low-level work will be allowed to pass through holes in the wall, under strict control and in return for more or less underhand, mafia-style payment.

It's interesting, this story of walls, under-stood as a guide to the story of worlds. The story of walls renders legible the story of worlds that assert unity only at the price of circumscribing within the world those elements that must remain external to it. This has been obvious since the time of fortresses, castles, walled cities, residential enclaves, colonial villas ... and it continues today. Let's go back to the 'fall' of the Berlin Wall. At the time, it was taken as a symbol that the unity of the world had finally been restored. There had been fifty years of separate worlds, of two explicitly different worlds: the socialist world and the capitalist world. When the 'socialist world' collapsed owing to its internal failures, its statism and the impossibility, despite Mao, of completing the communist 'Cultural Revolution', it was said that the 'totalitarian world' had been defeated by the 'democratic world'. The fall of the Berlin Wall was consequently the triumph of a single world, the world of democracy. But what we see today is that, where there were once two ideologically defined worlds, each of which acknowledged that there were two, today the wall has only shifted, it has only turned around. There has been a reorientation of the wall. Let's say that it stood between the socialist East and the capitalist

West, and now stands between what are collo-quially called the North and the South, meaning in fact: on the one hand the developing capitalist countries, including China, and on the other a whole series of 'zones' to be looted, whether in Africa, Asia, Latin America, or even Eastern and Southern Europe, where impoverished masses see commodities and monetary signs pass them by like lightning, beyond their reach.

Within the dominant countries themselves, the contradiction that the most elementary form of Marxism espoused, i.e. the impact of the internal division of worlds in these countries, was meant to set as strong and organised a working class as possible into opposition with the dominant bourgeoisie that controlled the state. But today the rich beneficiaries of world trade stand shoulder to shoulder with a considerable number of petty-bourgeois parasites, set against the enormous and growing mass of the excluded. 'Excluded' being the name for all those who in reality are not in the Western or democratic 'real world'; that is to say, those who are outside even if they are inside; the outside–inside. But perhaps a wall will be built to make it a little clearer that they are outside. It has already been made clear enough everywhere that there is a strong police presence patrolling the internal borders of the suburbs.

Such is the story of 'the world', or rather of 'worlds'. Until about 1980 there was an ideological wall, a political 'iron curtain' as we used to say; now there is a wall, multiform and growing, internal and external, to separate the enjoyment of the wealthy, and even that of the many semi-wealthy, from the desire of the poor and the ultra-poor. The way I see it, it is as if, in order for the single world of objects and monetary signs to exist, living bodies must be separated harshly according to their origins and the resources at their disposal. If the world of globalisation is the world of objects and signs, then living bodies must be separated. This is why I come to the conclusion that today there is no world. Because the unified world of capital comes at the price of the violent division of human existence into two regions separated by walls, police dogs, controls, naval patrols, barbed wire fences, and expulsions.

This is why the issue of so-called 'immigration', a very bad word for it, the issue of migrants, more correctly referred to as the issue of nomadic proletarians, has become a fundamental concern throughout the world. It is very striking that it has even become a concern in America, which for decades presented itself as the country of welcome and of immigration par excellence. Nowadays, even in America we hear of walls, controls, identification, and deportation. Every foreigner who arrives to live and work in rich countries, behind walls and police cordons, is proof that the thesis of the democratic unity of the world is completely false. They are the actual proof, the established proof, the living proof. Hence the pseudo-issue of 'immigrants' has become the bane of so-called 'democratic politics' in the false world of objects and signs.

Indeed, if the thesis of the democratic unity of the world were true, if, once the division of the world into two opposing ideological zones faltered, we had moved on to the democratic unity of the world, then we should be welcoming all these strangers as people from the same world as us. We should be greeting them as we would a traveller who stops by our house, with a 'Hi, how are you? Any news from home?' But we know that this is not what is happening. We, the unfortunate sedentary inhabitants of regions that have suffered the catastrophe of becoming capitals of the world of objects and signs, overwhelmingly consider that these people come from a different place.

They come from 'another world' within our own world. But if they come from another world it must be because, inside the world of objects and signs, another world exists. They are living proof that our democratic and developed world is not what it claims to be, namely the one world of living subjects, since there are women and men in our world who are considered to come from another world. Only money is the same everywhere. It knows nothing of two worlds: the dollar or the euro, the rouble or the yuan are the same everywhere, at home everywhere. Indeed, they alone are at home everywhere, to the extent that they can be exchanged against one another everywhere, regardless of their original provenance. We are happy enough to accept dollars or euros from someone who comes from another world. But in regard to their person, their origin, their way of existing, we say that they are not from our world. We place controls upon them, forbid them to stay, and anxiously ask ourselves how many of these people from another world are present in our house. A horrible question, one that inevitably paves the way for persecution, bans, and mass expulsions, if not worse. If the unity of the world is that of objects and monetary signs, for living bodies there is no unity of the world, there are zones, walls, desperate journeys, and deaths. This is why the central transcendental political question today is that of the world, of the existence of the world.

Many will say: 'True, true, but then we have to extend democracy, we just have to extend the good form of the world, the one that exists in the Western democracies and in Japan, everywhere. It's true, we need one world. It's unfortunate that we don't have it. But we need only extend the virtues of the true, good world to all the places where the bad world is found.' This vision is not only absurd, it is, as we shall increasingly come to realise, disastrous. For our democratic Western world has as its absolute material basis, its transcendental structure, the imposed circulation of objects and monetary signs. This is what constitutes its principal unity. And the fatal consequence of this is the separation of living bodies by the wealthy and the middle class, in the interests of the relentless defence of their privileges. Moreover, we know perfectly well what the concrete form of the extension of democracy is today: war – war in Iraq, in Afghanistan, in Somalia, in Africa. Terrible wars to 'extend democracy' to the rest of the world. Which is to say: to impose everywhere, by violence if need be, the possibility of being outside, outside-the-world, across vast zones of the falsely unified world.

As an aside, since an election is underway in France at the time of writing, I would like to say that if, in order to establish elections in the remote, deprived parts of the falsely unified world of objects and monetary signs, we have to wage terrible wars, this should lead us to reflect not only upon war but also upon elections. It should force us to ask ourselves to what concept of the world, to what theory of the world's existence, electoral democracy is linked today. This is a genuine question when we see that entire wars are legitimated solely on the basis that elections have been set up. We can see what happens: war, a war that destroys the country where the elections are held, a country that then disappears for decades into a kind of pseudo-electoral fever.

Basically, we have to accept the fact that, in the end, electoral democracy means the law of numbers, since it follows the model of what governs its reality, namely commodities and currencies. Voting is a law of counting, it is pseudo-political thought in calculable signs. Just as the world unified by the commodity imposes the law of money as the law of numbers, namely the price of things, and its real leaders are those who have the most money, so voting imposes the idea that the political winner is the one with the most votes. This brings us back to our problem: that if the world is one of objects and signs, then it is a world where everything is counted, where everything depends on the count. In politics, too, one must count, one must solicit votes and then count them. And as for those who don't count, or those who are not counted properly, we will impose our laws of countability upon them by military means, as in Baghdad and Libya. Just as we impose the price of products upon them, and have done so for a long time, through colonial war.

This proves, in my opinion, that the world of globalisation thus conceived does not exist as 'the' world, or if so only artificially, through violence alone. I therefore believe that we must turn the problem around and affirm, not as an observation, as a rule, but as an axiom, as a principle, the existence of the world, the existence of *a single* world. We must say this simple sentence, which seems trivial but which, as we have just seen, is not at all so: 'There is *one* world of living subjects.'

I insist that this sentence is not an objective conclusion, because we know that under the law of money there is not a single world of living subjects. There is the wall that separates, and there are people from a despised 'other world'. It has come to the point where, on the transcendental question, this phrase 'there is one world of living subjects' is in fact performative. It is not a statement but a prescription: we decide that it is so for us. We decide that we will be faithful to this declaration. And it's not a question of saying that we want to create such and such a world within the world as it is, it's not the immanent politics I spoke of, namely taking the world as it is and trying to steer it in a certain direction. No, no! It's a principle, an affirmative decision, a prescription: there is one world of living subjects. And we must exist in this world, a world that in a sense does not exist.

The problem consists in drawing the very harsh and difficult consequences of this simple sentence. In particular, to come back to the subject at hand, we must draw from this declaration of the unity of the world the existential assertions that it entails. The first consequence, which I think is fundamental for everyone, concerns those of foreign origin who live among us. If there is only one world of living subjects, it follows that those of foreign origin who live among us are of the same world as we are. Obviously, they cannot come from another world if prescriptively there is no other world. That's it – it's very simple. That African worker I see in the kitchen of the restaurant, the Moroccan I see digging a hole in the road, the veiled woman looking after the children in the park, they are all from the same world as me. This is a crucial point, which may not seem like much. But it is important because it is through this actual experience, through this inner declaration, that we overturn the transcendental organisation, the dominant idea that the world is unified only through signs and objects.

The unity of the world, then, is that of bodies. We must stand the test of this unity: these people who are here, different from me, are *there* (in the sense of being-there), that is, they exist *there*. They are different from me in language, clothing, religion, food, and education, and yet they exist in the same world. They exist, with their own degree of existence; they exist, in any case, in *the same way* that I do. It is not possible to register any qualitative difference in the principle of their existence. And, since they exist like me, I can, for example, talk with them, because one can talk with someone who is from the same world. As ever, there may be agreements and disagreements, but these don't have the same meaning when you assume that people are from the same world as they do when you assume that they are from another world. It's not the same system of agreements or disagreements, it's not the same system of distribution of intensities. The absolute condition of avoiding this is that *these people exist exactly like I do*, which means in the same world.

A number of objections will immediately arise here. The main objection is the one everyone talks about, namely cultural difference. After all, the whole world, the whole of my world, so they say, is the whole of those who have the same values as me, the whole of those for whom my values really stand. Those who are of the same world as me are those who are democrats, who respect women, who support human rights, etc. But as for those who have an opposing or different culture, they are not really democrats, they follow reactive religions, they have barbaric customs, they support despots, and they even have veiled women, and that's that. A small number of them may be allowed to enter our world (we're not animals, we need manpower for the dirty work), but only on condition that they learn our values and share them. And the key word here is 'integration'.

It is a word with a very strong speculative, or theoretical, or philosophical meaning: the term 'integration' means that, in order to enter the world that is ours, we must transform through education the principle of existence of 'immigrants', it means that these people must exist in such a way that they come into transcendental conformity with my existence. They do not exist as I do to start with, precisely because transcendental education is not the formalisation of an existence of the same kind as my own. 'Integration' is therefore quite precisely an assertion about the relationship between existence and the world. It is a certain conception of the relationship between the two: the person who comes from elsewhere must be integrated into our world; in other words, in order for the world of the African worker and our world (that of the masters of this world) to be the same, he, the African worker, must become the same as us, in a certain sense. If he is of the same world, then he is already the same as us, originally or axiomatically. But if this is not the case, if he has to learn our values, then that means that we maintain that he comes from elsewhere and that, in order to enter our world, in order for him to be the same, he has to *become* the same; he has to adopt the same practices, the same values.

You know that one of the presidential candidates of our republic said, to much applause, that if foreigners want to stay in France then they must love France, otherwise they must leave. Taking these statements at face value, I concluded that I should leave; because the France of the person who made this remark, and the person themselves, I don't like them at all and I don't share their so-called values at all. So I am not 'integrated' either.

It's clear that if you make it a condition that the African worker must be of the same world as you, then you ruin and abandon the principle that 'there is one world of living subjects'. Because, in order for there to be conditions set for sharing the world, it naturally has to be assumed that many others upon whom these conditions are imposed are from another world. So you have already abdicated the performative principle of 'there is only one world of living subjects'.

The last objection to the axiomatic thesis: 'There is only one world', which is of a slightly different order, is the fact that there are still laws in a country! And shouldn't a foreigner who is not from our country learn to obey our laws? That cannot be denied. Perhaps we might say that there will be no laws once communism has been achieved, once the state has withered away. But we are not asking for that much at the moment. Of course there are laws, but we must realise – and this is fundamental today – that a terrible confusion is taking place here between two things: laws and conditions. A law is not a condition. You don't integrate into a law. A law applies equally to everyone by definition. And a law therefore does not set conditions for belonging to a world. A law is a provisional rule that exists in a supposedly unique region of the world and, thank God, we don't ask anyone to like a law, we only ask them to obey it. Learning to obey laws is something that everyone has done in one way or another, and someone who comes from elsewhere will do it, and in this respect they are no different from anyone else.

The one world of living subjects, as we posit it axiomatically, may well require the newcomer to obey the laws on pain of police and judicial prosecution, like everyone else. However, this newcomer cannot be subjected to conditions of entry or existence that are evidently intended to control, forcibly orient, and potentially expel them. One cannot demand that in order to live in a single world, they must be like those who are already there, because that would be tantamount to saying that the only ones who belong to this world, axiomatically declared to be the only world, are those who are already in it, which is just a sham. And yet this imposture is the thesis that is implicitly supported today. Still less can one demand that they be like a minority of those who are already there, for example that they be strictly identical to the educated, democratic white petit bourgeois.

If there is only one world, then we must draw the consequences of this: all those who live in it exist in the same way as I do, transcendentally speaking, while not being like me, of course, precisely because existence is not being. They are not like me, they are different, but they exist like me – you can see that this difference between existence and being is necessary to get to the root of the question. The one world is precisely the place in which the infinity of differences exists, and it is the same world because those living in it are different in their existence. If, on the other hand, you ask those who live in the world to be the same, the world closes in on itself and becomes, as a world, distinct from another world. If you decree that there are conditions for being the same as you in the world, then you simultaneously decree that this world, your world, is different from another world. And this paves the way for separations, walls, controls, contempt, deaths, and ultimately war.

All of this leads to certain speculations about identities, which may be summarised as follows:

the world is populated by identities, but these identities are subject to the principle of existence, which is precisely where they vary. If you admit that there is only one world, you will at the same time admit that any identity is likely to be inscribed in distributions of different intensities. And so you are in no position to categorise identities. Identities are going to be involved in flexible becomings, which, if you look at them closely, always consist of two things. Firstly, an identity has an affirmative and creative dimension, which is the development, immanent to the world, of its invariance. This first aspect is the desire for my becoming to remain within the same – that is to say, for there to be a figure of the same within which my becoming can be inscribed. Ultimately this is a bit like when Nietzsche says: 'Become who you are' – it's about the immanent development of identity in a new situation. But an identity also has a negative or defensive dimension, which consists of separating one's identity from otherness, i.e. separating, distinguishing one's identity from that which is its other.

Let's take a very basic example. If there is only one world, then the Moroccan worker I was talking about earlier is in no way obliged to abandon what constitutes his individual, family, and collective identity. If there is only one world, then, like everyone else, he has differentiated traits of identity. What he will do, inevitably, is to adapt them little by little, in a creative way, to the place in which he finds himself, as anyone does in reality. That is to say, he's going to invent what he is, and that's why I quoted Nietzsche, namely, a Moroccan worker, yes, but one living in Aulnay-sous-Bois in France. He's going to invent that, an identity that didn't exist prior to his own existence, and he's going to exist in this particular figure of being a Moroccan worker in Aulnay-sous-Bois, in the general space of the one world of which he is one of the singular existences. He will in fact create himself as a subjective movement. He will go from the Moroccan peasant in the north of Morocco that he was to the worker living in a Paris suburb. He will appropriate this new figure of existence via what we might call a dilation of identity, such that his identity integrates possible displacements in a single world. This is the first dimension of identity, the one I call its creative dimension, within the horizon of the oneness of the world.

And it is absolutely unfair, and at the same time frightening, to demand that he do this in the form of an intimate break, a subjective break, an internal break.

This is hugely important, because the other way of asserting one's identity is negative, it truly is. It consists in defending, sometimes fiercely, one's insistence that 'I am not the other.' It could be defined as the refusal of integration. But, given what I think of integration, this refusal is a necessity. It is often necessary, this negative identity, especially when governments or reactionary opinion demand from you an authoritarian integration, a total negation of yourself. If this is the case, then you are justified in refusing to accept it. And this negative part of identity, which will simply consist of refusing what is demanded of you, namely to make an inner break with yourself, will make the dilation of identity impossible. As a result, this Moroccan worker, and maybe his children, will forcefully assert that their traditions and customs are not those of the European petty bourgeois; they will possibly emphasise further their religious or traditional traits of identity, and they will phantasmatically oppose the

Western world, whose superiority they do not accept.

I wanted to show by this that in identity conceived as a principle of existence, remembering precisely that 'existence' and 'identity' are distinct and in a complex dialectical play with one another, there are two ways of asserting identity in its difference, as experienced in a zone of the one world that the subject does not yet know. There is an affirmative use of identity: the Same maintains itself by inventing an appropriation of the new place. In this case it is a creation, which I call the dilation of identity into the transcendental of the one world. And then there is a negative use: the Same defends itself against its forced authoritarian corruption by the other, it seeks to preserve what it calls its 'purity'. One could say that any identity, constituted transcendentally as existence in one world, is always the dialectical interplay of a movement of creation and a movement of purification, regardless of the identity concerned.

This allows us to move towards an understanding of the relationship between identities or identity-based forms of existence, and the great principle that 'there is only one world'.

The general idea is simple enough: if we uphold axiomatically, in principle, the unity of the world of living subjects, then identities will assert creation over purification, the dilation of identity over defensive formulas. When the opposite happens, it is because in reality it is not prescriptively assumed that there is one world, but constantly signified that there are many and that people come from all manner of other places. It is always under these conditions that purification gains the upper hand over creation. This is why the politics of walls, persecution, control, and expulsions is a disaster. A serious disaster, the frightening consequences of which we have not yet explored in full. It is a disaster because it creates two imaginary worlds and, by affirming in everything it does that there are two worlds, it comes to deny the existence of humanity and paves the way for infinite wars. It even makes the rot set in within our own societies. Because the Moroccans, the Malians, the Senegalese, the Bangladeshis, and all the others, they will still come, and in large numbers. And the persecution will reinforce the purification process in them; that is to say, in the face of Western governments that demand immediate authoritarian integration, it is certain that we will have to deal with young Islamists ready to martyr themselves for the purity of their faith. And the counter-effect will be to transform our societies into repressive and police societies. All of this is well underway already and is set to continue.

The only way to fight this process is to declare axiomatically that there is only one world, and to argue that the internal consequences of this axiom are necessary political actions that help open up the creative aspect of identities. As I said, this is what is permanently underway at the École des Actes, which, in the Théâtre de la Commune, welcomes newcomers and old-timers alike, and its maxim could be summarised as follows: to do everything possible to ensure that the creative aspect of identity prevails over conservatism; that the faithful creation of identity prevails over the purification that only opposes the other; that through various collective teachings, through general assemblies where every word is translated into all of the languages represented in the room, through the provision of constant aid against all the identity-reactive provocations invented by the state and nationalists of all stripes, it should be affirmed by all: 'We together, all different, inhabit one and the same world.'

Let's sum all of this up in four points:

– Firstly, we posit that the world of unbridled capitalism is a false world; that is, it recognises only the unity of markets and monetary signs and therefore expels the majority of humanity into another devalued world, from which it separates itself by walls and war. In this sense, today, and from, if I may say so, an objective point of view, there is not *a* world.

– Secondly, to affirm that 'there is one world' is a principle of action, a categorical imperative of true politics. This principle is that of the equality of existences in all places of this one world.

– Thirdly, the principle of the existence of one world does not contradict the infinite play of identities and differences, it only entails that identities subordinate their negative dimension to their affirmative dimension, subordinating opposition to others to the immanent and varied development of the Same.

– Fourthly, with regard to the existence of hundreds of thousands of foreigners in our countries, there are three joint objectives: to oppose persecutory integration, to limit reactive purification, and to develop or expand creative identity. I think that the articulation of these three objectives defines what we can call today 'a politics', 'a politics of the world', or 'a politics of existence in regard to the world'.

In the early 1980s, a French Socialist Prime Minister said: 'Immigrants are a problem.' He even added: 'This is proof that Le Pen poses the right problems, but proposes the wrong solutions.' Within the horizon of the one-world question, we can reverse this verdict and say: 'Foreigners are an opportunity, a chance to solve the problems of our one world. A radical chance, not merely an empirical or secondary one, but a chance that touches on the very essence of a possible true politics.'

Finally, the mass of foreign workers, their children, the second, third or fourth generation, to what do they testify in our old and somewhat tired countries? They bear witness to the youth of the world, to its breadth, to its infinite variety, rather than to absurd stories of fences, cultures, and integrations. It is with this youth that the politics of the future will be invented. Truth is always something that begins in figures of foreignness. It is the variability of existence in the unity of the world that is the natural milieu of all figures of creative thought. If we don't keep this idea in mind, we will fall into the twofold trap of nihilistic consumption and police order. Because this is the duality that constitutes the world we are being promised: nihilistic consumption and police order, which go together perfectly.

If true existence is precisely the gap between one identity and another, the creative difference of identity, then let us allow foreigners at least to teach us to become a little bit foreign to ourselves. To no longer entirely be prisoners of a long, white, Western history. Let's face it, this history is coming to an end, and will do so with or without our help. If we insist on perpetuating it, it will only bring sterility and war. I think that, on the assumption that there is only one world of existence and identity, we must welcome foreignness as such – that is, existence as re-evaluated by ourselves. Because that is what foreignness is: the re-evaluation of existence. And we can say that, thus conceived in the element of foreignness, all true politics (through its new topology, through its new figures of the distribution of intensities) is like a kind of new dawn of existence. And we can also say, rather than harping on in defence of the long history that is coming to an end: Let us greet this dawn! Yes, let us greet this dawn. In the one world no longer ruled by fallacious principles, foreignness is really the dawning of existence, in politics as elsewhere.